I0213312

GRACE HARLOWE'S SOPHOMORE YEAR AT HIGH SCHOOL

or

The Record of the Girl Chums in Work and Athletics

JESSIE GRAHAM FLOWER, A.M.

1st WORLD LIBRARY Literary Society

Grace Harlowe's Sophomore Year at High School

Jessie Graham Flower

© 1st World Library, 2006
PO Box 2211
Fairfield, IA 52556
www.1stworldlibrary.com
First Edition

LCCN: 2006907730

Softcover ISBN: 1-4218-2432-9
Hardcover ISBN: 1-4218-2332-2
eBook ISBN: 1-4218-2532-5

Purchase *"Grace Harlowe's Sophomore Year at High School"*
as a traditional bound book at:
www.1stWorldLibrary.com/purchase.asp?ISBN=1-4218-2432-9

1st World Library is a literary, educational organization
dedicated to:

- Creating a free internet library of downloadable ebooks

  - Hosting writing competitions and offering book
    publishing scholarships.

Interested in more 1st World Library books?
contact: literacy@1stworldlibrary.com
Check us out at: www.1stworldlibrary.com

1st World Library Literary Society

Giving Back to the World

"If you want to work on the core problem, it's early school literacy."

- James Barksdale, former CEO of Netscape

"No skill is more crucial to the future of a child, or to a democratic and prosperous society, than literacy."

- Los Angeles Times

Literacy... means far more than learning how to read and write... The aim is to transmit... knowledge and promote social participation."

- UNESCO

"Literacy is not a luxury, it is a right and a responsibility. If our world is to meet the challenges of the twenty-first century we must harness the energy and creativity of all our citizens."

- President Bill Clinton

"Parents should be encouraged to read to their children, and teachers should be equipped with all available techniques for teaching literacy, so the varying needs and capacities of individual kids can be taken into account."

- Hugh Mackay

CONTENTS

CHAPTER I

A DECLARATION OF WAR

"Anne, you will never learn to do a side vault that way. Let me show you," exclaimed Grace Harlowe.

The gymnasium was full of High School girls, and a very busy and interesting picture they made, running, leaping, vaulting, passing the medicine ball and practising on the rings.

In one corner a class was in progress, the physical culture instructor calling out her orders like an officer on parade.

The four girl chums had grown somewhat taller than when last seen. A rich summer-vacation tan had browned their faces and Nora O'Malley's tip-tilted Irish nose was dotted with freckles. All four were dressed in gymnasium suits of dark blue and across the front of each blouse in letters of sky-blue were the initials "O.H.S.S." which stood for "Oakdale High School Sophomore." They were rather proud of these initials, perhaps because the lettering was still too recent to have lost its novelty.

"Never mind," replied Anne Pierson; "I don't believe I shall ever learn, it, but, thank goodness, vaulting isn't entirely necessary to human happiness."

"Thank goodness it isn't," observed Jessica, who never really enjoyed gymnasium work.

"It is to mine," protested Grace, glowing with exercise and enthusiasm. "If I couldn't do every one of these stunts I should certainly lie awake at night grieving over it."

She gave a joyous laugh as she vaulted over the wooden horse as easily and gracefully as an acrobat.

"I'd much rather dance," replied Anne. "Ever since Mrs. Gray's Christmas party I've wanted to learn."

"Why Anne," replied Grace, "I had forgotten that you don't dance. I'll give you a lesson at once. But you must first learn to waltz, then all other dancing will be easy."

"Just watch me while I show you the step," Grace continued.

"Now, you try it while I count for you."

"One, two, three. One, two, three. That's right. Just keep on practising, until you are sure of yourself; then if Jessica will play for us, I'll waltz with you."

"With pleasure," said Jessica, "Anne must learn to waltz. Her education in dancing mustn't be neglected another minute."

Anne patiently practised the step while Jessica played a very slow waltz on the piano and Grace counted for Anne. Then the two girls danced together, and under Grace's guidance Anne found waltzing wasn't half as hard as she had imagined it would be.

By this time the gymnasium was almost empty. The class in physical culture had been dismissed, and the girls belonging to it had withdrawn to the locker rooms to dress and go home. The four girl chums were practically alone.

"I do wish the rest of the basketball team would put in an appearance," said Grace, as she and Anne stopped to rest. "We need every minute we can get for practice. The opening game is so very near, and it's really difficult to get the gymnasium now, for the juniors seem to consider it their especial possession. One would think they had leased it for the season."

"They are awfully mean, I think," said Nora O'Malley. "They weren't at all nice to us last year when we were freshmen and they were sophomores. Even the dignity of being juniors doesn't seem to improve them any. They are just as hateful as ever."

"Most of the juniors are really nice girls, but it is due to Julia Crosby that they behave so badly," said Jessica Bright thoughtfully, "She leads them, into all kinds of mischief. She is a born trouble-maker."

"She is one of the rudest girls I have ever known," remarked Nora with emphasis. "How Miriam Nesbit can tolerate her is more than I can see."

"Well," said Grace, "it is hardly a case of toleration. Miriam seems really fond of her."

"Hush!" said Anne, who had been silently listening to the conversation. "Here comes the rest of the team, and Miriam is with them."

Readers of the preceding volume of this series, "GRACE HARLOWE'S PLEBE YEAR AT HIGH SCHOOL," need no introduction to Grace Harlowe and her girl chums. In that volume was narrated the race for the freshman prize, so generously offered each year by Mrs. Gray, sponsor of the freshman class, and the efforts of Miriam Nesbit aided by the disagreeable teacher of algebra, Miss Leece, to ruin the career of Anne Pierson, the brightest pupil of Oakdale High School. Through the loyalty and cleverness of Grace and her friends, the plot was brought to light and Anne was vindicated.

Many and varied were the experiences which fell to the lot of the High School girls. The encounter with an impostor, masquerading as Mrs. Gray's nephew, Tom Gray, the escape from wolves in Upton Woods, and Mrs. Gray's Christmas ball proved exciting additions to the routine of school work.

The contest between Grace and Miriam Nesbit for the basketball captaincy, resulting in Grace's subsequent election, was also one of the interesting features of the freshman year.

The beginning of the sophomore year found Miriam Nesbit in a most unpleasant frame of mind toward Grace and her friends. The loss of the basketball captaincy had been a severe blow to Miriam's pride, and she could not forgive Grace her popularity.

As she walked across the gymnasium followed by the other members of the team, her face wore a sullen expression which deepened as her eyes rested upon Grace, and she nodded very stiffly to the young captain. Grace, fully aware of the coldness of Miriam's salutation, returned it as courteously as though Miriam had been one of her particular friends. Long before this Grace had made up her mind to treat Miriam as though nothing disagreeable had ever happened. There was no use in holding a grudge.

"If Miriam once realizes that we are willing to overlook some things which happened last year," Grace had confided to Anne, "perhaps her better self will come to the surface. I am sure she has a better self, only she has never given it a chance to develop."

Anne did not feel quite so positive as to the existence of Miriam's better self, but agreed with Grace because she adored her.

The entire team having assembled, Grace lost no time in assigning the players to their various positions.

"Miriam will you play one of the forwards?" she asked.

"Who is going to play center?" queried Miriam ignoring Grace's question.

"Why the girls have asked me to play," replied Grace.

"If I cannot play center," announced Miriam shrugging her shoulders, "I shall play nothing."

A sudden silence fell upon the group of girls, who, amazed at Miriam's rudeness, awaited Grace's answer.

Stifling her desire to retort sharply, Grace said? "Why Miriam, I didn't know you felt that way about it. Certainly you may play center if you wish to. I am sure I don't wish to seem selfish."

This was too much for Nora O'Malley, who deeply resented Miriam's attitude toward Grace.

"We want our captain for center," she said. "Don't we, girls?"

"Yes," chorused the girls.

It was a humiliating moment for proud Miriam. Grace realized this and felt equally embarrassed at their outspoken preference.

Then Miriam said with a contemptuous laugh, "Really, Miss Harlowe, I congratulate you upon your loyal support. It is a good thing to have friends at court. However, it is immaterial to me what position I play, for I am not particularly enthusiastic over basketball. The juniors are sure to win at any rate."

A flush mounted to Grace's cheeks at Miriam's insulting words. Controlling her anger, she said quietly:

"Very well, I will play center." Then she rapidly named the other players.

This last formality having been disposed of, the team lined up for practice. Soon the game was at its height. Miriam in the excitement of the play, forgot her recently avowed indifference toward basketball and went to work with all the skill and activity she possessed.

The basketball team, during its infancy in the freshman class had given splendid promise of future fame. Grace felt proud of her players as she stopped for a moment to watch their agile movements and spirited work. Surely, the juniors would have to look out for their laurels this year. Her blood quickened at thought, of the coming contests which were to take place during the course of the winter between the two class teams. There were to be three games that season, and the sophomores had made up their minds to win all of them. What if the junior team were a famous one, and had won victory after victory the year before over all other class teams? The sophomores resolved to be famous, too.

In fact, all of Grace's hopes were centered on the coming season. Napoleon himself could not have been more eager for victory.

"We must just make up our minds to work, girls," she exhorted her friends. "I would rather beat those juniors than take a trip to Europe."

Nor was she alone in her desire. The other girls were just as eager to overthrow the victorious juniors. It was evident, so strong was the feeling in the class, that something more than a sense of sport had stirred them to this degree of rivalry.

The former freshman class had many scores against the present juniors. As sophomores, the winter before, they had never missed an opportunity to annoy and irritate the freshmen in a hundred disagreeable ways. "The Black Monks of Asia" still rankled in their memories. Moreover, was not Julia Crosby, the junior captain? She was the same mischievous sophomore who had created so much havoc at the Christmas ball. She was always playing unkind practical jokes on other people. It is true, she was an intimate and close friend of Miriam Nesbit, but they all were aware that Miriam was a law unto herself, and none of them had ever attempted to explain certain doings of hers in connection with Julia Crosby and her friends during the freshman year.

Grace's mind was busy with these thoughts when the door of the gymnasium opened noisily. There was a whoop followed by cries and calls and in rushed the junior players, most of them dressed in gymnasium suits.

Julia Crosby, at their head, had come with so much force, that she now slid halfway across the room, landing right in the midst of the sophomores.

"I beg your pardon," said Grace, who had been almost knocked down by the encounter, "I suppose you did not notice us. But you see, now, that we are in the midst of practising. The gym. is ours for the afternoon."

Julia Crosby looked at her insolently and laughed.

How irritating that laugh had always been to the rival class of younger girls. It had a dozen different shades of meaning in it - a nasty, condescending contemptuous laugh, Grace thought, and such qualities had no right to be put in a laugh at all, since laughing is meant to show pleasure and nothing else. But Julia Crosby always laughed at the wrong time; especially when there was nothing at which to laugh.

"Who said the gym. was yours for the afternoon?" she asked.

"Miss Thompson said so," answered Grace. "I asked her, this morning, and she gave us permission, as she did to you last Monday, when the boys were all out at the football grounds."

"Have you a written permission?" asked Julia Crosby, laughing again, so disagreeably that hot-headed Nora was obliged to turn away to keep from saying something unworthy of herself.

"No," answered Grace, endeavoring to be calm under these trying circumstances, but her voice trembling nevertheless with anger. "No, I have no written permission and you had none last Monday. You know as well as I do that the boys principal is willing to lend us the gym. as often as we like during football season, when it is not much in use; and that Miss Thompson tries to divide the time as evenly as possible among the girls."

"I don't know anything about that, Miss Harlowe," said Julia Crosby. "But I do know that you and your team will have to give up the gymnasium at once, because our team is in a hurry to begin practising."

Then a great chattering arose. Every sophomore there except Miriam Nesbit raised a protesting voice. Grace held up her hand for silence, then summoning all her dignity she turned to Julia Crosby.

"Miss Crosby," she said, "you have evidently made a mistake. We have had permission to use the gymnasium this afternoon, which I feel sure you have not had. It was neither polite nor kind to break in upon us as you did, and the least you can do is to go away quietly without interrupting us further."

"Really, Miss Harlowe," said Julia Crosby, and again her tantalizing laugh rang out, "you are entirely too hasty in your supposition. As it happens, I have the best right in the world to bring my team to the gym. This afternoon. So, little folks," looking from one sophomore to another in a way that was fairly maddening, "run away and play somewhere else."

"Miss Crosby," cried Grace, now thoroughly angry, "I insist on knowing from whom you received permission. It was not granted by Miss Thompson."

"Oh, I did not stop at Miss Thompson's. I went to a higher authority. Mr. Cole, the boys' principal, gave me a written permission. Here it is. Do you care to read it?" and Julia thrust the offending paper before Grace's eyes.

This was the last straw. Grace dashed the paper to the floor, and turned with flashing eyes to her tormentor.

"Miss Crosby," she said, "if Professor Cole had known that Miss Thompson had given me permission to use the gymnasium, he would never have given you this paper. You obtained it by a trick, which is your usual method of gaining your ends. But I want you to understand that the sophomore class will not tamely submit to such impositions. We evened our score with you as freshmen, and we shall do it again this year as sophomores. Furthermore, we mean to win every basketball game of the series, for we should consider being beaten by the juniors the deepest possible disgrace. I regret that we have agreed to play against an unworthy foe."

With her head held high, Grace walked from the gymnasium, followed by the other members of her team, who were too indignant to notice that Miriam had remained behind.

CHAPTER II

THE WAY OF THE TRANSGRESSOR

Once outside the gymnasium, Grace's dignity forsook her, and she felt a wild desire to kick and scream like a small child. The contemptible conduct of the junior team filled her with just rage. With a great effort at self-control she turned to the other girls, who were holding an indignation meeting in the corridor.

"Girls," she said, "I know just how you feel about this, and if we had been boys there would have been a hand-to-hand conflict in the gymnasium to-day."

"I wish we hadn't given in," said Nora, almost sobbing with anger.

"There was really nothing else to do," said Anne. "It is better to retire with dignity than to indulge in a free-for-all fight."

"Yes," responded Grace, "it is. But when that insufferable Julia Crosby poked Professor Cole's permit under my nose, I felt like taking her by the shoulders and shaking her. What those juniors need is a good, sound thrashing. That being utterly out of the question, the only thing to do is to whitewash them at basketball."

"Three cheers for the valiant sophomores!" cried Nora, "On to victory! Down with juniors!"

The cheers were given with a will, and by common consent the crowd of girls moved on down the corridor that led to the locker room.

The sophomore locker room was the particular rendezvous of that class in general. Here matters of state were discussed, class gossip retailed, and class friendships cemented. It was in reality a sort of clubroom, and dear to the heart of every girl in the class. To the girls in their present state of mind it seemed the only place to go. They seated themselves on the benches and Grace took the floor.

"Attention, fellow citizens and basketball artists," she called. "Do you solemnly promise to exert yourselves to the utmost to repay the juniors for this afternoon's work?"

"We do," was the answer.

"And will you pledge your sacred honor to whip the juniors, no matter what happens!"

"We will," responded the girls.

"Anne!" called Grace. "You and Jessica are not players, but you can pledge your loyalty to the team anyhow. I want you to be in this, too. Hold up your right hands."

"We will be loyal," said both girls, holding up their right hands, laughing meanwhile at Grace's serious expression.

"Now," said Grace, "I feel better. As long as we can't get the actual practice this afternoon let's lay out a course of action at any rate, and arrange our secret signals."

"Done," cried the girls, and soon they were deep in the mysteries of secret plays and signs.

Grace explained the game to Anne, who did not incline towards athletics, and had had little previous opportunity to enjoy them.

Anne, eager to learn for Grace's sake, became interested on her own account, and soon mastered the main points of the game.

"Here is a list of the secret signals, Anne," said Grace. "Study it carefully and learn it by heart, then you will understand every move our team makes during the coming games. I expect you to become an enthusiastic fan."

Anne thanked her, and put the paper in her purse, little dreaming how much unhappiness that same paper was to cause her.

The business of the afternoon having been disposed of, the girls donned street clothing and left the building, schoolgirl fashion, in groups of twos and threes.

On the way out they encountered several of the victorious juniors, who managed to make their presence felt.

"Oh," said Nora O'Malley, "those girls ought to be suppressed."

"Never mind," put in Anne. "You know 'the way of the transgressor is hard.' Perhaps those juniors will get what they deserve yet."

"Not much danger of it. They're too tricky," said Jessica contemptuously.

Anne's prophecy was to be fulfilled, however, in a most unexpected manner.

There had been one unnoticed spectator of the recent quarrel between the two classes. This was the teacher of physical culture, Miss Kane, who had returned to the gymnasium for a moment, arriving just in time to witness the whole scene. She, too, had had trouble at various times with the junior class, particularly Julia Crosby, who invariably tried her patience severely. She had been heard to pronounce them the most unruly class she had ever attempted to instruct. Therefore her sympathies were with the retreating sophomores, and with set lips and righteous indignation in her eye, she resolved to lay the matter before Miss Thompson, at the earliest opportunity.

Miss Thompson listened the next day with considerable surprise to Miss Kane's account of the affair. No one knew the mischievous tendencies of the juniors better than did the principal. Ordinary mischief she could forgive, but this was overstepping all bounds. She had given the sophomore class permission to use the gymnasium for the afternoon, and no other class had the least right to take the matter over her head. She knew that Professor Cole was entirely innocent of the deception practised upon him, so she resolved to say nothing to him, but deal with the junior team as she deemed best. One thing was certain, they should receive their just deserts.

Miss Thompson's face, usually calm and serene, wore an expression of great sternness as she faced the assembled classes in the study-hall the following morning. The girls looked apprehensively at each other, wondering what was about to happen. When their beloved principal looked like that, there was trouble brewing for some one. Miss Thompson, though a strict disciplinarian, was seldom angry. She was both patient and reasonable in her dealings with the pupils under her supervision, and had their utmost confidence and respect. To incur her displeasure one must commit a serious offense. Each girl searched her mind for possible delinquencies There was absolute silence in the great room. Then the principal spoke:

"I must ask the undivided attention of every girl in this room, as what I am about to say relates in a measure to all of you.

"There are four classes, representing four divisions of high school work, assembled here this morning. Each one must be passed through before the desired goal - graduation - is reached.

"The standard of each class from freshmen to seniors, should be honor. I have been very proud of my girls because I believed that they would be able to live up to that standard. However it seems that some of them have yet to learn the meaning of the word."

Miss Thompson paused. Nora cast a significant look toward Jessica, who sat directly opposite her, while Julia Crosby fidgeted nervously in her seat, and felt suddenly ill at ease.

"Good-natured rivalry between classes," continued Miss Thompson, "has always been encouraged, but ill-natured trickery is to be deplored. A matter has come to my ears which makes it necessary for me to put down with an iron hand anything resembling such an evil.

"You are all aware that I have been very willing to grant the use of the gymnasium to the various teams for basketball practice, and have tried to divide up the time as evenly as possible. Two days ago I gave the members of the sophomore team permission to use the gymnasium for practice. No other team had any right whatever to disturb them, yet I understand that another team did commit that breach of class etiquette, drove the rightful possessors from the room and occupied it for the remainder of the afternoon. The report brought to me says that the young women of the sophomore team conducted themselves with dignity during a most trying situation."

Miss Thompson turned suddenly toward the junior section.

"The members of the junior basketball team will please rise," she said sternly.

There was a subdued murmur throughout the section, then one after another, with the exception of Julia Crosby, the girls rose.

"Miss Crosby," said the principal in a tone that brooked no delay, "rise at once! I expect instant obedience from every pupil in this school."

Julia sulkily rose to her feet.

"Miss Crosby," continued Miss Thompson, "are you not the captain of the junior team?"

"Yes," answered Julia defiantly.

"Did you go to Professor Cole for permission to use the gymnasium last Thursday?"

"Yes."

"Why did you not come to me?"

Julia hung her head and made no reply.

"I will tell you the reason, Miss Crosby," said the principal. "You already knew that permission had been granted the sophomore team, did you not?"

"Yes," said Julia very faintly.

"Very well. You are guilty of two serious misdemeanors. You purposely misrepresented matters to Professor Cole and deliberately put aside my authority; not to mention the unwomanly way in which you behaved toward the sophomore team. Every girl who aided and abetted you in this is equally guilty. Therefore you will all learn and recite to me an extra page in history every day for two weeks. The use of the gymnasium will be prohibited you for the same length of time, and if such a thing ever again occurs, the culprits will be suspended without delay. You may be seated."

The dazed juniors sank limply into their seats. The tables had been turned upon them with a vengeance. A page of history a day was bad enough, but the loss of the gymnasium privilege was worse. The opening game was only two weeks off, and they needed practice.

Julia Crosby put her head down on her desk and wept tears of rage and mortification. The rest of the girls looked ready to cry, too.

The first bell for classes sounded and the girls picked up their books. At the second bell they filed out through the corridor to their various recitation rooms. As Grace, who had stopped to look for a lost pencil, hurried toward the geometry classroom, she passed Julia Crosby, who was moping along, wiping her eyes with her handkerchief. Julia cast an angry glance at Grace, and hissed, "tale-bearer."

Grace, inwardly smarting at the unjust accusation walked on without answering.

"What did I tell you about the way of the transgressor?" said Anne to Grace, as they walked home from school that day.

"It certainly is hard enough this time," said Grace. "But," she added, as she thought of Julia Crosby's recent accusation, "the way of the righteous isn't always easy."

CHAPTER III

A GENEROUS APPEAL

The juniors themselves hardly felt the weight of their punishment more than did Grace Harlowe. Her heart was set on winning every basketball game of the series. But she wished to win fairly and honestly. Now, that the juniors had been forbidden the use of the gymnasium, the sophomores might practise there to their heart's content. But was that fair? To be sure the juniors had deserved their punishment, but what kind of basketball could they play after having had no practice for two weeks? Besides, Julia Crosby blamed her for telling what had occurred in the gymnasium. She had gone to Julia, earnestly avowing innocence, but Julia had only laughed at her and refused to listen.

All this passed rapidly through Grace's mind as she walked toward the High School several mornings later. Something must be done, but what she hardly knew. The game could be postponed, but Grace felt that the other girls would not care to postpone it. They were heartily glad that the junior team had come to grief, and showed no sympathy for them.

"There's just one thing to be done," sighed Grace to herself. "And that's to go to Miss Thompson and ask her to restore the juniors their privilege. I hate to do it, she was so angry with them. But I'll do what I can, anyway. Here goes."

Miss Thompson was in her office when Grace entered rather

timidly, seating herself on the oak settee until the principal should find time to talk to talk with her.

"Well, Grace, what can I do for you?" said Miss Thompson, looking up smilingly at the young girl. "You look as though you carried the cares of the world upon your shoulders this morning."

"Not quite all of them, but I have a few especial ones that are bothering me," replied Grace. Then after a moment's hesitation she said, "Miss Thompson, won't you, please, restore the juniors their gymnasium privilege?"

Miss Thompson regarded Grace searchingly. "What a peculiar request to make, Grace. Don't you consider the juniors' punishment a just one?"

"Yes," said Grace earnestly, "I do. But this is the whole trouble. The first basketball game between the juniors and the sophomores is scheduled to take place in less than two weeks. If the juniors do not practise they will play badly, and we shall beat them. We hope to win, at any rate, but we want to feel that they have had the same chances that we have had. If they do fail, they will say that it was because they had no opportunity for practice. That will take all the sweetness out of the victory for us."

"I think I see," said Miss Thompson, smiling a little. "It is a case of the innocent suffering with the guilty, isn't it? Personally, I hardly feel like restoring these bad children to favor, as they sadly needed a lesson; but since you take the matter so seriously to heart; I suppose I must say 'yes.'"

"Thank you so much, dear Miss Thompson," said Grace with shining eyes, "and now I want to ask one more favor. Julia Crosby believes that I reported her to you that day. Of course you know that I did not. Will you please tell her so? Her accusation has made me very unhappy."

Miss Thompson looked a trifle stern. "Yes, Grace," she said, "I will attend to that, too."

Grace turned to go, but Miss Thompson said. "Wait a moment, Grace, I will send for Miss Crosby."

Julia Crosby heard the summons with dismay. She wondered what Miss Thompson could have to say to her. The principal's reprimand had been so severe that even mischievous Julia felt obliged to go softly. Another performance like the last might cut short her High School career. So she let the sophomores severely alone. She was, therefore, surprised on entering the office to meet Grace Harlowe face to face.

"Miss Crosby," said Miss Thompson coldly, "Miss Harlowe has just asked me to restore the junior team their gymnasium privilege. Had any other girl asked this favor I should have refused her. But Miss Harlowe, in spite of the shabby way in which she has been treated, is generous enough to overlook the past, and begs that you be given another chance. It is only for her sake that I grant it.

"Also, Miss Crosby, I received no information from Miss Harlowe or any of her team regarding your recent rude conduct in the gymnasium. The report came from an entirely different source. You may go; but first you may apologize to Miss Harlowe, and thank her for what she has done."

With a very poor grace, Julia mumbled a few words of apology and thanks and hurried from the room. The principal looked after her and shook her head, then turning to Grace, she asked, "Well, Grace, are you satisfied?"

Grace thanked her again, and with a light heart sped towards the study hall. Once more she could look forward to the coming game with pleasant anticipations.

Julia Crosby had already informed the junior players of the rise in their fallen fortunes. When school was over they gathered about their leader to hear the story. Now, Julia, if possible felt more bitter toward Grace than formerly. It galled her to be compelled to accept anything from Grace's hands, and she did not intend to let any more of the truth be known than she could help. This was too good an opportunity to gain popularity to let slip through her fingers So she put on a mysterious expression and said:

"Now, see here, girls, I got you into all that trouble, and I made up my mind to get you out again. Just go ahead and practise for all your worth, and don't worry about how it all happened."

"Well," said Alice Waite, "it was awfully brave of you to go to Miss Thompson, even if you are too modest to tell of it. Wasn't it, girls?"

"Yes," chorused the team. "Three cheers for our brave captain."

Julia, fairly dazzled at her own popularity, smiled a smile of intense satisfaction. She had produced exactly the impression that she wished.

"What on earth are those juniors making such a fuss about?" inquired Nora O'Malley, as the four chums strolled across the campus toward the gate. The junior team, headed by Julia, was coming down the walk talking at the top of their voices.

"Nothing of any importance, you may be sure," said Jessica Bright. "'Shallow brooks babble loudest,' you know."

"They seem to be 'babbling' over Julia Crosby just now," said Anne, who had been curiously watching the jubilant juniors.

"No doubt she has just unfolded some new scheme," said Nora sarcastically, "that will be practised on the sophomores at the first opportunity."

"Doesn't it seem strange," said Grace, who had hitherto offered no comments, "that we must always be at sixes and sevens with the juniors? Such a spirit never existed between classes before. I wonder how it will all end?"

"Don't worry your dear head over those girls, Grace," said Anne, patting Grace's hand. "They aren't worth it."

"Oh, look girls!" exclaimed Nora suddenly. "There is David Nesbit, and he is coming this way. I haven't seen him for an age."

"Good afternoon, girls," said David, lifting his cap. "It is indeed a pleasure to see you."

"Why, David," said Grace, "you are quite a stranger. Where have you been keeping yourself?"

Anne also looked her pleasure at seeing her old friend.

"I have been very, very busy with some important business of my own," said David in a mock-pompous tone. Then he announced: "I am going to give a party and I am going to invite all of you. Will you come?"

"We will!" cried Nora. "Dressed in our costliest raiment, at that."

"Never mind about the fine clothes," said David, laughing. "This is to be a plain, every-day affair."

"Who else is invited, David?" asked Jessica.

"Only one other girl beside yourselves has had the honor of receiving an invitation."

"Miriam?" queried Grace, unable to conceal a shade of disappointment in her tone.

"No, no; not Miriam," answered Miriam's brother.

Grace looked relieved. If Miriam joined the party, something unpleasant was sure to happen. Miriam treasured a spite against Anne for winning the freshman prize, and never treated her with civility when they chanced to meet. Grace knew, too, that Miriam's attitude toward her was equally hostile. She wondered if David knew all these things about his sister.

Whatever he did know of Miriam and her deep-laid plans and schemes, he divulged to no one. None of the girls had ever heard him say a word against his sister; although they felt that he deeply disapproved of her jealousy and false pride.

"You haven't guessed her name yet," smiled David. "She is one of my best friends, girls. She has been my sweetheart ever since I was a young man of five. She's one of the prettiest girls in Oakdale, she's sixty years young, and her name is -"

"Dear Mrs. Gray, of course!" exclaimed Grace delightedly.

"And has she accepted your invitation?" asked Anne.

"She has," replied David, "and will come in her coach and four, or rather her carriage and two. You ordinary mortals will be obliged to walk, I fear."

"But why does she use her 'coach and four,' When she lives in the palace just next door?" rhymed Nora.

"Very good, my child," commented David. "However, what I was about to say was this: My party is not to be in a house. It is an open-air party. We are to meet at the Omnibus House, to-morrow afternoon at four o'clock. Two very distinguished gentlemen have also been invited - Mr. Reddy Brooks and Mr. Hippy Wingate."

A shout of laughter went up from the girls

"Distinguished, indeed," cried Nora. "It will be a delightful party I am sure."

"Shall we bring food for Hippy!"

"No," laughed David. "Let him eat the apples he finds on the ground. If we feed him on every festive occasion he will soon be too fat to walk, and we shall have to roll him about on casters."

"What a terrible fate," said Anne smiling.

"Well, girls? do you promise to attend?"

"Yes? indeed!" cried the four girls.

"Be sure not to surprise us with a disappointment."

"The main thing is not to disappoint you with the surprise," were his parting words.

"If all boys were as nice as David the world would be a better place!" exclaimed Grace. "I suppose you can guess what the object of this party is."

"Never mind, don't mention it," said Jessica in a low tone. "Here come some other girls, and if they knew what we know, there would be a multitude instead of a select, private party at the Omnibus House to-morrow."

CHAPTER IV

AN UNFORTUNATE AVIATOR

It was an unusual entertainment that David had provided for his little circle of intimate friends in the old orchard surrounding the Omnibus House. There was a look of intense excitement in his eyes, as he stood awaiting his guests, the following afternoon. Mrs. Gray had already arrived, and, leaving her carriage to wait for her near the entrance, now stood by David and helped him receive.

"It's good to see all my children together again," she exclaimed, giving Anne a gentle hug; for ever since her Christmas house party she had acquired a sort of proprietary feeling toward these young people. "I only wish Tom Gray were to be with us to-day. I should like him to have a share in the surprise; for you may be sure there is to be a surprise. David would never have asked us to this lonely place for nothing."

"David is a good old reliable, Mrs. Gray," cried Hippy. "Certainly if I had imagined for a moment that he would disappoint us, I never should have dragged my slight frame all this distance."

"Good, loyal old Hippy," replied David. "The surprise is ready, but even if it had not been, there is no exercise so beneficial to stout people as walking."

"Well, bring it on, bring it on," exclaimed Reddy. "We are waiting patiently."

"Curb your impatience, Sorrel Top," said David. "Just follow me, and see what I have to show you."

They helped little Mrs. Gray, who was nimble in spite of her years, through a broken gap in the wall of the Omnibus House. The old ruin was more picturesque than, ever in its cloak of five-leafed ivy which the autumn had touched with red and gold. A lean-to had been built against the back wall of the building, fitted with a stout door on the inside and a pair of doors on the outside.

"I rented this plot of land from the farmer who owns the orchard," explained David, taking a key from his pocket and opening the door in the stone wall. "This was about the best place I could think of for experiments, partly because it's such a lonesome place, and partly because there is a clear open space of several hundred yards back here without a tree or bush on it."

It was dark inside until he had opened the double doors in the opposite wall, when the slanting light showed them an aeroplane; not a little gymnasium model this time, but a full-fledged flying machine, a trim and graceful object, even at close view.

"David," cried Anne joyously, "you don't mean to say you've gone and done it at last?"

"I have," answered David gravely; "and I've made two trips with pretty good success each time."

Then everyone talked at once. David was the hero of the hour.

"David, my dear boy," cried Mrs. Gray. "To think that I should live to see you an aviator!"

"I'm a long way from being one, yet, Mrs. Gray," answered David. "My bird doesn't always care to fly. There are times when she'd rather stay in her nest with her wings folded. Of course, I haven't nearly perfected her yet, so I don't want it mentioned in town until I get things in shape. But I couldn't wait until then to show it to you, my dear friends, because you were all interested in it last year."

"Well, well, come on and fly," cried Hippy. "My heart is palpitating so with excitement that I am afraid it will beat once too often if something doesn't happen."

"I was waiting for my helper," answered David, "but he appears to be late. You boys will do as well."

"Who is your helper, David?" asked Anne.

"You could never guess," he replied smiling, "so I'll have to tell you. It's old Jean, the hunter."

"Why, the dear old thing!" cried Grace. "To think of him leaving his uncivilized state to do anything so utterly civilized and modern as to help with a flying machine."

"And he does it well, too," went on David. "He is not only thoroughly interested but he keeps guard out here in case any one should try to break in. There are his cot and things in the corner. He sleeps in the open unless it rains. Then he sleeps inside."

As the old hunter did not put in an appearance David decided to wait no longer.

"Why can't we all help?" asked Grace. "What must we do? Please tell us."

"All right," answered David, "just give it a shove into the open space, and you'll see how she gradually rises for a flight."

After making a careful examination of all the parts of the aeroplane, and starting the engine, David took his seat in the machine.

Then the two boys, assisted by Grace and Nora, pushed it swiftly out into the broad open space back of the ruin.

Suddenly the machine began to rise. Slowly, at first, then seeming to gather strength and confidence like a young bird that has learned to fly at last, it soared over the apple trees. David, white, but very calm, quietly worked the levers that operated the little engine. When he had risen about a hundred feet, he began to dip and soar around the orchard in circles. He appeared to have forgotten his friends, watching anxiously below. He did not notice that little Mrs. Gray's knees had suddenly refused to support her, nor that she had sat flat on the ground in a state of utter bewilderment at the sight of his sudden flight. David looked far across at the beautiful rolling meadows, and fields dotted with farmhouses and cottages. How he loved the fertile valley, with its little river winding in and out between green banks! It was all so beautiful, but it was time to descend. He must not give his pet too much liberty, or he might rue his indiscretion. He headed his machine for the open space back of the Omnibus House, and began the descent. Then, something snapped, and he fell. He remembered as he fell the look of horror on the up-raised faces of his friends, and then everything became a blank.

It all happened in a flash, much too quickly to do anything but stand and wait until the aeroplane had crashed to the ground, but it seemed much longer, and Anne remembered later that she had felt a curious impulse to run away and hide. If David were to meet his death through this new toy, she could not endure to stay and see it happen.

But David was far from dead. He was only stunned and dizzy from the swift descent. He had not been high enough from the ground when the accident occurred to sustain serious injuries. They lifted him from the machine and laid him upon the grass, while Reddy ran to the brook and brought back his cap filled with water.

Mrs. Gray produced her smelling salts which she always carried with her. "Not for my own use, my dears," she always said, "but for the benefit of other people."

Reddy loosened David's collar and dashed the water into his face; while Hippy chafed the unconscious boy's wrists.

Presently David opened his eyes, looking vaguely about. He had a confused idea that something had happened to him, but just what it was he could not think. He looked up into the anxious faces of his friends who stood around him. Then he remembered.

"I'm not hurt," he said in a rather weak voice. Then he sat up and smiled feebly at the company. "I just had the wind knocked out of me. I am sure no bones are broken. How about my pet bird? Has she smashed her little ribs?"

"No, old fellow," exclaimed Hippy in a reassuring tone, for Hippy had never been able to endure the sight of suffering or disappointment. "Her wings are a good deal battered, that's all. But are you all right, old man?" he added, feeling David's arms and legs, and even putting an ear over his heart.

"It's still beating, you foolish, old fat-head," said David, patting his friend affectionately on the back.

In the meantime Anne had helped Mrs. Gray to her feet.

"I declare, I feel as though I had dropped from the clouds myself," said the old lady, wiping her eyes. "I am so stunned and bewildered. David, my dear boy, if you had been seriously hurt I should never have forgiven myself for allowing you to fly off like that. What would your poor mother say if she knew what had happened?"

"It won't be necessary to break the news to her, Mrs. Gray," said David. "I shall be as good as new inside of a few minutes. It's my poor little bird here who has received the injuries. Look at her poor battered wings! I think I know just what caused my sudden descent though, and I'll take care it doesn't happen again."

David then began a minute examination of his damaged pet, and soon located the trouble. His friends listened, deeply interested, as he explained the principles of aviation, and showed them how he had carried out his own ideas in constructing his aeroplane. Grace, who had a taste for mechanics, asked all sorts of questions, until Hippy asked her if she intended building an aeroplane of her own.

"I may," replied Grace, laughing. "You know that girls have as much chance at the big things of the world to-day, as boys."

"Well, if you do, let me know," responded Hippy, "and I'll write an epic poem about you that will make the world sit up and take notice."

"Then I am assured of fame beforehand," laughed Grace.

"Look!" said Nora suddenly. "Who are those people coming across the orchard? Doesn't that look like Julia Crosby and some of her crowd?"

"Yes," exclaimed Grace, "it is, and Miriam is with them."

"Then help me get my aeroplane into the shed quickly," exclaimed David. "You know that the Crosby girl is not a favorite with me." Then he added half to himself, "I don't see why Miriam insists on going around with her so much."

The boys lost no time in getting the aeroplane into the house, David slammed the doors, and triumphantly turned the key in the lock just as Miriam and her party came up.

With a quick glance Miriam's eyes took in the situation. She bowed courteously to Mrs. Gray, whom she dared not slight; included Grace, Nora and Jessica in a cool little nod, and stared straight past Anne. Then turning to her brother she said, "David, show Miss Crosby and her friends your aeroplane, they wish to see it."

A look of grim determination settled about David's mouth. Looking his sister squarely in the face, he said, "I am sorry to seem disobliging but I cannot show your friends my aeroplane and I am surprised to find that they know I have one."

Miriam reddened at this, but said insolently, "If you can invite other people to see it, you can show it to us."

There was an uncomfortable silence. Mrs. Gray looked surprised and annoyed. The peaceful old lady, disliked scenes of any kind. Grace and her chums, knowing that Miriam was only making herself ridiculous, felt embarrassed for her. Then Julia Crosby laughed in her tantalizing irritating way.

That settled the matter as far as David was concerned.

"You are right," he said, "I could show my flying machine to you and your friends if I cared to do so. However, I don't care to. Knowing that I wished my experiment to be kept a secret, you came here with the one idea of being disagreeable, and you have succeeded. I am sorry to be so rude to my own sister, but occasionally the brutal truth is a good thing for you to hear, Miriam."

Miriam was speechless with anger, but before she could frame a reply, Mrs. Gray said soothingly "Children, children don't quarrel. David, it is getting late. We had better go. I suppose it is of no use to ask any of you athletic young folks to ride back to town." With a little bow to Miriam and her discomfited party, Mrs. Gray turned toward where her carriage awaited her, followed by David and his friends.

Jessie Graham Flower

After bidding her good-bye, the young people took the road to town. For David's sake all mention of the recent unpleasantness was tacitly avoided, though it was uppermost in each one's mind.

"I have one thing to be thankful for," said Grace to Anne, as she turned in at her own gate, "and that is that Miriam Nesbit isn't my sister."

As for Miriam, her feelings can be better imagined than described. She sulked and pouted the whole way home, vowing to get even with David for daring to cross her. Julia Crosby grew rather tired of Miriam's tirade, and left her with the parting advice that she had better forget it.

When Miriam reached home she immediately asked if David had come in. Receiving an affirmative reply, she went from room to room looking for him, and finally found him in the library. He was busy with a book on aviation. She snatched the book from him, threw it across the room and expressed her opinion of himself and his friends in very plain terms. Without a word David picked up his book and walked out of the library, leaving her in full possession of the field.

CHAPTER V

ON THE EVE OF BATTLE

But little time remained before the first basketball game of the series between the sophomores and juniors. Both teams had been untiring in their practice. There had been no further altercations between them as to the use of the gymnasium, for the juniors, fearing the wrath of Miss Thompson, were more circumspect in their behavior, and let the sophomore team strictly alone.

"They are liable to break out at any time, you can trust them just as far as you can see them and no farther, and that's the truth," cried Nora O'Malley. The sophomore players were standing in the corridor outside the gymnasium awaiting the pleasure of the juniors, whose practice time was up.

"They are supposed to be out of here at four o'clock," continued Nora, "and it's fifteen minutes past four now. They are loitering on purpose They don't dare to do mean things openly since Miss Thompson lectured them so, but they make up for it by being aggravating."

"Never mind, Nora," said Grace, smiling at Nora's outburst. "We'll whip them off the face of the earth next Saturday."

"Well, I hope so," said Nora, "I am sure we are better players."

"What outrageous conceit," said Jessica, and the four girls

Jessie Graham Flower

laughed merrily.

"By the way, Grace," said Anne, "I want to ask you something about that list you gave me. I don't quite understand what one of those signals means."

"Trot it out," said Grace. "I'll have time to tell you about it before the practice actually begins."

Anne took out her purse and began searching for the list. It was not to be found.

"Why, how strange," she said. "I was looking at it this morning on the way to school. I wonder if I have lost it. That would be dreadful."

She turned her purse upside down, shaking it energetically, but no list fell out.

"Oh, never mind," said Grace, seeing Anne's distress. "It's of no consequence. No one will ever find it anyway. Suppose it were found, who would know what it meant?"

"Yes, but one would know," persisted Anne, "because I wrote 'Sophomore basketball signals' on the outside of it. Oh, dear, I don't see how I could have been so careless."

"Poor little Anne," said Jessica, "she is always worried over something or other."

"Now see here, Anne," said Grace, "just because you lost a letter last term and had trouble over it, don't begin to mourn over those old signals. No one will ever see them, and perhaps you haven't lost them. Maybe you'll find them at home."

"Perhaps I shall," said Anne brightening.

"Now smile Anne," said Nora, "and forget your troubles. There is no use in crossing bridges before you come to them."

This homely old saying seemed to console Anne, and soon she was eagerly watching the work of the team, her brief anxiety forgotten.

That night she searched her room, and the next day gave her desk in school a thorough overhauling, but the list of signals remained missing.

The sophomore players with their substitute team met that afternoon in the gymnasium. It was their last opportunity for practice. Saturday they would rise to victory or go down in ignominious defeat. The latter seemed to them impossible. They had practised faithfully, and Grace had been so earnest in her efforts to perfect their playing that they were completely under her control and moved like clockwork. There was no weak spot in the team. Every point had been diligently worked over and mastered. They had played several games with the freshmen and had won every time, so Grace was fairly confident of their success.

"Oh, girls," she cried, wringing her hands in her earnestness, "don't make any mistakes. Keep your heads, all of you. I am convinced we are better players than the juniors, even if they did get the pennant last year. For one thing I don't think they work together as well as we do, and that's really the main thing. Miriam, you missed practice yesterday. You are going to stay to-day, aren't you?"

Miriam nodded without replying. She was busy with her own thoughts. She wished she could hit upon some way to humiliate Grace Harlowe. But what could she do? That was the question. The members of the team adored their gray-eyed, independent young captain, therefore she would have to be very careful.

She had been steadily losing ground with her class on account of her constant association with the juniors, and the slightest misstep on her part would jeopardize her place on the team. She had a genuine love for the game, and since she couldn't play on the junior team, she concluded it would be just as well not to lose her place with the sophomores. In her heart she cared nothing for her class. She had tried to be their leader, and Grace had supplanted her, but now Grace should pay for it.

All this passed through Miriam's mind as she covertly watched Grace, who was reassuring Anne for the fiftieth time, not to worry over the lost signals.

"Don't tell any one about it," she whispered to Anne. "You may find them yet."

Anne shook her head sorrowfully. She felt in some way that those signals were bound to make trouble for her.

"By the way, girls," said Grace, addressing the team, "has any one any objection to Anne and Jessica staying to see the practice game? They have seen all our work and are now anxious to see the practice game. They know all the points, but they want to see how the new signal code works."

"Of course not," answered the girls. "We won't turn Oakdale's star pupil out of the gym. Anne shall be our mascot. As for Jessica, she is a matter of course."

"I object," said Miriam. "I object seriously."

"Object?" repeated Grace, turning in amazement to Miriam. "Why?"

"You know that it is against all basketball rules to allow any one in the gymnasium during practice except the regular team and the subs. If we follow our rules then we shall be certain that nothing we do reaches the ears of the juniors. We have always made an exception of Jessica, but I don't think we should allow any one else here."

"And do you think that Anne Pierson would carry

information?" exclaimed Grace sharply. "Really, Miriam, you are provoking enough to try the patience of a saint. Just as if Anne, who is the soul of honor, would do such a thing."

An indignant murmur arose from the girls. They were all prepared to like little Anne, although they did not know her very well.

"How can you say such things, Miriam?" cried Nora.

"I didn't say she would," said Miriam rather alarmed at the storm she had raised. "But I do think it is better to be careful. However, have it your own way. But if we lose the game -"

She paused. Her judgment told her she had said enough. If anything did happen, the blame would fall on Grace's shoulders.

Anne, deeply hurt, tried to leave the gymnasium but the girls caught her, and brought her back again. She shed a few tears, but soon forgot her grief in the interest of the game.

"Girls," said Grace, as she and Nora and Jessica walked down the street that night after leaving Anne at her corner, "we must look out for Anne. It is evident from the way Miriam acted to-day that she will never lose an opportunity to hurt Anne's feelings. I thought perhaps time would soften her wrath, but it looks as though she still nursed her old grudge."

How true Grace's words were to prove she could not at that time foresee.

"Well," said Nora, "Anne is one of the nicest girls in Oakdale, and if Miriam knows when she's well off she'll mind her own business."

The day before the game, as Grace was leaving school, she heard David's familiar whistle and turned to see the young man hurrying toward her, a look of subdued excitement upon his face.

"I've been looking all over for you, Grace," he said, as he lifted his cap to her. "I have something to tell you. This afternoon after school, Reddy, Hippy and I went out to the old Omnibus House. I wanted to show the fellows some things about my machine. While we were out there who should appear but Julia Crosby and some more of her crowd. They were having a regular pow-wow and were in high glee over something. We kept still because we knew if they saw us they'd descend upon us in a body. They stayed a long time and Julia Crosby made a speech. I couldn't hear what she said, but it seemed to be about the proper thing, for her satellites applauded about every two minutes. Then they got their heads together and all talked at once. While they were so busy we skipped out without being noticed. I thought I'd better tell you, for I have an idea they are putting up some scheme to queer you in the game to-morrow; so look out for them."

"Thank you, David," answered Grace. "You are always looking after our interests. I wonder what those juniors are planning. They are obliged to play a fair game, for they know perfectly well what will happen if they don't. Miss Thompson will be there to-morrow, and they know she has her eye on them."

"Put not your trust in juniors," cautioned David. "They may elude even her watchful eye."

"You are coming to see us play to-morrow, aren't you, David?" asked Grace.

"I'll be there before the doors are open, with Reddy and Hippy at my heels," responded David. "Good-bye, Grace. Look out for squalls to-morrow."

CHAPTER VI

THE DEEPEST POSSIBLE DISGRACE

A feeling of depression swept over Grace Harlowe as she looked out the window the next morning. The rain was falling heavily and the skies were sullen and gray.

"What a miserable day for the game," was her first thought. "I do hope the rain won't keep people away. This weather is enough to discourage any one."

All morning she watched anxiously for the clouds to lift, going from window to door until her mother told her to stop fretting about the weather and save her strength for the coming game.

The game was set for two o'clock, but at one, Grace put on her raincoat and set out for the High School. She knew she was early, but she felt that she couldn't stay in the house a minute longer.

One by one the sophomore team and its substitutes assembled, but the rain had dampened their spirits and the enthusiasm of the past few days had left them.

Grace looked worried, as she noticed how listless her players seemed. She wished it had been one of those cold, crisp days that set the blood tingling and make the heart beat high with hope.

Still Grace felt confident that her team would rise to the occasion when the game was called. They were two well-trained, too certain of their powers to ever think of failing.

The bad weather had evidently not depressed the spirits of their opponents. The juniors stood about laughing and talking. Julia Crosby moved from one girl to the other whispering slyly.

"Wretch!" thought Grace. "How disagreeable she is. She was born too late. She should have lived in the middle ages, when plotting was the fashion. She is anything but a credit to her class and dear old Oakdale High School."

Grace's rather vehement reflections were cut short by the approach of Miss Thompson, who stopped to say a word of cheer to the girls before taking her seat in the gallery.

"Well, Grace," she said, "this is a rather bad day outside, but still there will be a few loyal souls to cheer you on to victory. May the best man win. You must put forth every energy if you expect to conquer the juniors, however. They have held the championship a long time."

"They will not hold it after to-day if we can help it," answered Grace. "We feel fairly sure that we can whip them."

"That is the right spirit," said Miss Thompson. "Confidence is first cousin to success, you know."

"Was there ever a teacher quite like Miss Thompson?" asked Nora as the principal left them to take her seat in the gallery.

"She is a dear," said Marian Barber, "and she's on our side, too."

"There's the referee now!" exclaimed Grace. "Now, girls, make up your minds to play as you never played before. Remember it's for the honor of the sophomores."

By this time the gallery was half filled with an audience largely composed of High School boys and girls. A few outsiders were present. Mrs. Harlowe had come to see her daughter's team win the game, she said; for she knew that Grace's heart was set on victory.

The referee, time-keeper and scorer chosen from the senior class took their places. The whistle blew and the teams lined up. There was a round of loud applause from the fans of both teams. The players presented a fine appearance. The earnest, "do or die" expression on every face made the spectators feel that the coming game would be well worth seeing.

The rival captains faced each other, ready to jump for the ball the instant it left the referee's hands. There was a moment of expectant silence; then the referee put the ball in play, the whistle blew and the game began. Both captains sprang for the ball, but alas for the sophomores, Julia Crosby caught it and threw it to the junior right forward. It looked for a minute as though the juniors would score without effort, but Nora O'Malley, who was left guard, succeeded so effectually in annoying her opponent that when the bewildered goal-thrower did succeed in throwing the ball, it fell wide of the basket. It had barely touched the floor before there was a rush for it, and the fun waxed fast and furious.

During the first five minutes neither side scored; then the tide turned in favor of the juniors and they netted the ball.

Grace Harlowe set her teeth, resolving to play harder than ever. The juniors should not score again if she could help it. Nora had the ball and was dribbling it for dear life. Grace signaled her team, who responded instantly; but, to their consternation, the juniors seemed to understand the signal as fully as did their own team, and quickly blocking their play, scored again.

There was a howl of delight from the junior fans in the gallery. The sudden triumph of the enemy seemed to daze the sophomores. They looked at their captain in amazement, then sprang once more to their work. But the trend the game was taking had affected them, and in their desperate efforts to score they made mistakes. Miriam Nesbit ran with the ball and a foul was called, which resulted in the juniors scoring a point.

Nora O'Malley, in her excitement, caught the forward she was guarding by the arm, and again a foul was called; this time, however, the juniors made nothing from it. But the precious time was flying and only four minutes of the first half remained. Again Grace signaled for another secret play, and again the juniors rose to the occasion and thwarted her.

It was maddening.

The score stood 7 to 0 in favor of the juniors. Miriam Nesbit had the ball now, and was trying to throw it. She stood near the junior basket. Eluding her guard, who was dancing about in front of her, she made a wild throw. Whether by accident or design it was hard to tell, but the ball landed squarely in the junior basket. A whoop went up from the gallery. The whistle blew and the first half was over. The score stood 9 to 0 in favor of the enemy. The last two points had been presented to the juniors.

Up in the gallery discussion ran rife. The admirers of the juniors were loud in their praise of the superior ability of the team. The junior class, who were sitting in a body at one end of the gallery, grew especially noisy, and were laughing derisively at the downfall of the sophomores.

Miss Thompson was puzzled.

"I cannot imagine what ails my sophomores," she said to the teacher next to her. "I understood that they were such fine players. Yet they don't seem to be able to hold their own. It looks as though their defeat were inevitable, unless they do some remarkable playing during the next half."

Mrs. Harlowe, too, was disappointed. She wondered why Grace had boasted so much of her team.

"After all, they are little more than children," she thought. "Those juniors seem older to me."

As for Grace and her team - they were sitting in a room just off the gymnasium gloomily discussing the situation. Tears of mortification stood in Nora's eyes, while Grace was putting forth every effort to appear calm. She knew that if she showed the least sign of faltering all would be lost. Her players must feel that she still had faith in their ability to win.

"We are not beaten yet, girls," she said, "and I believe we shall make up in the last half what we lost in the first. Work fast, but keep your wits about you. Don't give the referee any chance to call a foul, we can't spare a minute from now on. When I give the signal for a certain play, be on the alert, and please, please don't any of you present those juniors with any more points. I'm not blaming you, Miriam, for I know that last throw of yours was an accident, but I could have cried when that ball went into the basket."

Miriam's face flushed; then realizing that all eyes were turned toward her, she said sarcastically:

"Really, Miss Harlowe, it's so kind of you to look at it in that light. However, anyone with common sense would have known without being told that I never intended that ball for the juniors."

"I am not so sure of that," muttered Nora, who, seeing the hurt look that crept into Grace's eyes at Miriam's words, immediately rose in behalf of her captain.

Miriam whirled on Nora.

"What did you say?" asked Miriam angrily.

Jessie Graham Flower

Before Nora could answer the whistle blew. Intermission was over and the second half was on. The teams changed baskets and stood in readiness for work. Once more Grace and Julia Crosby faced each other. There was a malicious gleam in Julia's eye and a look of determination in Grace's. With a spring, Grace caught the ball as it descended and threw it to Nora, who, eluding her guard, tossed it to Miriam. With unerring aim Miriam sent the ball into the basket and the sophomores scored for the first time.

Their friends in the gallery applauded vigorously and began to take heart, but their joy was short-lived, for as the play proceeded the sophomores steadily lost what little ground they had gained. Try as they might, they could make no headway. Grace called for play after play, only to find that in some inexplicable way the enemy seemed to know just what she meant, and acted accordingly.

The game neared its close and the sophomores fought with the desperation of the doomed. They knew that they could not win save by a miracle, but they resolved to die hard. The ball was in Miriam's hands and she made a feint at throwing it to Nora, but whirled and threw it to Grace, who, divining her intention, ran forward to receive it. There was a rush on the part of the juniors. Julia Crosby, crossing in front of Grace, managed slyly to thrust one foot forward. Grace tripped and fell to the floor, twisting one leg under her. The ball rolled on, and was caught by the enemy, who threw it to goal just as the whistle sounded for the last time. The juniors had won. The score stood 17 to 2 in their favor. The scorer attempted to announce it, but her voice was lost in the noisy yells of the junior class in the gallery.

The fact that Grace Harlowe still sat on the gymnasium floor passed for a moment unnoticed. In the final grand rush for the ball, the other players failed to see that their valiant captain still occupied the spot where she fell. Tumbles were not infrequent, and Grace was well able to take care of herself.

Anne Pierson alone saw Julia Crosby's foot slide out, and, scenting treachery, hastily left her seat in the gallery. She ran as fast as she could to where Grace sat, reaching her a few seconds after the w histleblew.

"Good little Anne," called Grace. "You have come to my rescue even though the others have deserted me. Perhaps you can help me up. I tried it, but my ankle hurts every time I try to stand."

Her face was very white, and Anne saw that she was in great pain.

By this time Grace's team, realizing she was not with them, began looking about, and rushed over to her in a body. David, Reddy and Hippy appeared on the scene, as did Mrs. Harlowe, accompanied by Miss Thompson. Excitement reigned. The boys lifted Grace to her feet; but she cried with pain and would have fallen had they not held her.

"She has sprained her ankle!" exclaimed Miss Thompson. "How did it happen, Grace? I did not see you fall."

"I don't know, Miss Thompson," said Grace faintly. "It all happened so quickly I didn't have time to think about it."

"It certainly is a shame," cried Anne. "And I know -"

Just then Grace gave Anne a warning glance and shook her head slightly. Anne closed her lips and was silent.

"What were you saying, Anne?" asked Miss Thompson.

But Anne had received her orders.

"I am so sorry that Grace has been hurt," she said lamely.

A carriage was ordered and Grace was taken home, Anne and Mrs. Harlowe accompanying her. Mrs. Harlowe sent for their physician, who bandaged the swollen ankle, and told Grace that the sprain was not serious. She refused, however, to go to bed, but lay on the wide lounge in the sitting room.

"Just keep quiet for a few days, and you'll be all right," said Dr. Gale. "You girls are as bad as boys about getting hard knocks. It looks as though basketball were about as barbarous as football."

"It is a dear old game, and I love it in spite of hard knocks," said Grace emphatically.

"I like your spirit, Grace," laughed Dr. Gale. "Now, remember to treat that ankle well if you want to appear again in the basketball arena."

"Grace," said Anne, after the doctor had gone. "You know how it happened, don't you?"

"Yes," answered Grace, after a little hesitation. "I do."

"What are you going to do about it?" asked Anne.

"I don't know," said Grace. "I am not sure it was intentional."

"Grace," said Anne with decision, "it was intentional. I watched her every minute of the game, for I didn't trust her, and I saw her do it. I was so angry that when Miss Thompson asked how it happened I felt that I must tell, then and there. It was you who prevented me. I think such a trick should be exposed."

"What a vengeful little Anne," said Grace. "You are usually the last one to tell anything."

She took Anne's hand in hers.

"It's just this way, Anne," she continued. "If I were to tell what Julia Crosby did, Miss Thompson might forbid basketball.

That would be dreadful. Besides, the juniors would hardly believe me, and would say it was a case of sour grapes, on account of the sophomores losing the game. So you see I should gain nothing and perhaps lose a great deal. I believe that people that do mean things are usually repaid in their own coin. Julia didn't really intend to hurt me. Her idea was to prevent me from getting the ball. Of course it was dishonorable and she knew it. It is strictly forbidden in basketball, and if her own team knew positively that she was guilty, it would go hard with her. There is honor even among thieves, you know."

There was a brief silence. Grace lay back among the cushions, looking very white and tired. Her ankle pained her severely, but the defeat of her beloved team was a deeper hurt to her proud spirit.

Anne sat apparently wrapped in thought. She nervously clasped and unclasped her small hands.

"Grace," she said, "don't you think it was queer the way the juniors seemed to understand our signals. They knew every one of them. I believe that they found that list and it is all my fault. I had no business to lose it. I felt when I couldn't find it that it would fall into the wrong hands and cause trouble. I don't care for myself but if the girls find it out they will blame you for giving it to me. You know what Miriam said the other day. Now she will have a chance to be disagreeable to you about it."

Anne was almost in tears.

"Anne, dear," said Grace soothingly, "don't worry about it. I am not afraid to tell the girls about that list, and I shall certainly do so. They will understand that it was an accident, and overlook it. Besides, we are not sure that the juniors found it. I will admit that everything points that way. You know David warned us that they had some mischief on hand. If they did find it, the only honorable thing to do was to return it.

They are far more at fault than we are, and the girls will agree with me, I know."

But Anne was not so confident.

"Miriam will try to make trouble about it, I know she will. And I am to blame for the whole thing," she said.

Grace was about to reply when Mrs. Harlowe appeared in the door with a tray of tempting food.

Anne rose and began donning her wraps.

"Won't you stay, Anne, and have supper with my invalid girl?" said Mrs. Harlowe.

"Please do, Anne," coaxed Grace. "I hate eating alone, and having you here takes my mind off my pain."

Anne stayed, and the two girls had a merry time over their meal. Grace, knowing Anne's distress over the lost signals, refused to talk of the subject. Jessica and Nora, David, Hippy and Reddy dropped in, one after the other, to inquire for Grace.

"There is nothing like accidents to bring one's friends together," declared Grace, as the young people gathered around her.

"I told you to look out for squalls, Grace," said David. "But you didn't weather the gale very well."

"Those juniors must have been eavesdropping when you made your signal code. They understood every play you made. By George, I wonder if that were the meaning of that pow-wow the other day. Some one must have put Julia Crosby wise, and that's why she called a meeting at the Omnibus House. It's an out-of-the-way place, and she thought there was no danger of being disturbed.

"Who could have been mean enough to betray us?" cried Nora. "I am sure none of the team did, unless -" Nora stopped short.

She had been on the point of using Miriam's name, but remembered just in time that Miriam's brother was present.

"If we knew the girl who did it, we'd certainly cut her acquaintance," said Reddy Brooks.

"Never again should she bask in the light of our society," said Hippy dramatically.

"None of our friends would do such a thing," said David soberly. Then, turning to Anne, "What's your opinion on the subject, Queen Anne?"

But Anne could find no answer. She simply shook her head.

Grace, knowing Anne's feelings over the affair, came to the rescue.

"Anne's opinion and mine are the same. We feel sure that they knew our signals, but we believe they accidentally hit upon the knowledge. There is no use in crying over spilt milk. We shall have to change all our signals and take care that it doesn't happen again. And now let's talk of something more agreeable, for basketball is a sore subject with me in more than one sense." The talk drifted into other channels much to Anne's relief.

"I have an idea!" exclaimed Hippy.

"Impossible," said Reddy. "No one would ever accuse you of such a thing."

"Be silent, fellow," commanded Hippy. "I will not brook such idle babbling." He strutted up and down the room, his chest inflated and one hand over his heart, presenting such a ridiculous figure that he raised a general laugh.

"Speak on, fat one. I promise not to make any more remarks," said Reddy.

"I propose," said Hippy, pausing in his march, "that we give an impromptu vaudeville show for the benefit of Miss Grace Harlowe, once an active member of this happy band, but now laid on the shelf - couch, I mean - for repairs."

"Done," was the unanimous reply.

"Now," continued Hippy, "get cozy, and the show will begin. Miss Nora O'Malley will open the show by singing 'Peggy Brady,' as only an Irish colleen of her pretensions can."

Nora rose, looked toward Jessica, who went at once to the piano to accompany her, and sang the song demanded with a fascinating brogue that always brought forth the applause of her friends. She responded to an encore. Then Anne's turn came, and she recited "Lasca." Hippy next favored the company with a comic song, which caused them to shout with laughter. Jessica did her Greek dance for which she was famous. The performance ended with an up-to-date version of "Antony and Cleopatra," enacted by David, Reddy and Hippy, with dialogue and stage business of which Shakespeare never dreamed.

It was a product of Hippy's fertile brain, and the boys had been rehearsing it with great glee, in view of appearing in it, on some fitting occasion, before the girls.

David, gracefully draped in the piano cover, represented Egypt's queen, and languished upon Marc Antony's shoulder in the most approved manner. Reddy, as the Roman conqueror left nothing to be desired. The star actor of the piece, however, was Hippy, who played the deadly asp. He writhed and wriggled in a manner that would have filled a respectable serpent with envy, and in the closing scene bit the unfortunate Cleopatra so venomously that she howled for mercy, and instead of dying gracefully, arose and engaged in battle with his snakeship.

Grace forgot her sprained ankle and laughed until the tears rolled down her cheeks.

"You funny, funny boys," she gasped, "how did you ever think of anything so ridiculous!"

"Hippy perpetrated the outrage," said David "and we agreed to help him produce it. We have been practising it for two weeks, only we don't generally end up with a scuffle. I hope you will pardon us, Grace, but the desire to shake that husky Egyptian reptile was irresistible."

"There is nothing to pardon," replied Grace, "and we have only thanks to offer for the fun you have given us."

"It was indeed a notable performance," agreed Nora.

"Girls and boys," said Anne, "it is almost ten o'clock and Grace ought to be in bed. I move that we adjourn."

"Second the motion," said David. "We have been very selfish in keeping poor Grace up when she is ill."

"Poor Grace is glad you came, and isn't a bit tired," replied Grace, looking fondly at her friends. "You must all come to see me as often as you can while I am laid up. I shall be pretty lonely for a few days."

The young folks departed, singing "Good Night, Ladies" as they trooped down the walk.

"What a pleasure it is to have such dear, good friends," thought Grace as she lay back on her couch after they had gone. "They are well worth all the loyalty I can give them."

She went to sleep that night unconscious of how soon her loyalty to one of them would be put to the test.

CHAPTER VII

GATHERING CLOUDS

"A sprained ankle is not so serious," declared Grace from her nest among the sofa cushions. It was the Monday after the game. Her various sympathetic classmates were seated about the Harlowe's comfortable living room. A wood fire crackled cheerfully in the big, open fireplace, while a large plate of chocolate fudge circulated from one lap to another.

"Jessica, will you pour the chocolate?" continued Grace to her friend, who rose at once to comply with her request. "Anne, will you help serve, please?"

Anne accordingly drew about the room a little table on wheels, containing on its several shelves plates containing sandwiches, cookies and cakes.

"Trust to the Harlowe's to have lots of good things to eat," exclaimed Marian Barber. "It must be fun to be laid up, Grace, if you can give a party every afternoon."

"I must entertain my friends when they are kind enough to come and see me," answered Grace. "But some people think sandwiches poor provender unless they are the fancy kind, with olives and nuts in them. Miriam, for instance would never serve such plain fare to her company as cream cheese sandwiches."

"Here comes Miriam up the walk now," cried Jessica. "She looks as though she had something on her mind."

Presently the door opened and Miriam was ushered in. Grace wondered a little at her call, considering the unfriendly spirit Miriam had recently exhibited toward her. She greeted Miriam cordially. The laws of hospitality were sacred in the Harlowe family, and not for worlds would Grace have shown anything but the kindest feeling toward a guest under her own roof.

Miriam accepted the chair and the cup of chocolate tendered her, ignoring the plate of cakes offered by Anne. She looked about her like a marksman taking aim before he fires. There was a danger signal in either eye.

"She is out for slaughter," thought Nora.

"Well, Miriam, what's the news?" said Marian Barber good-naturedly. "You have a mysterious, newsy look in your eye. Is it good, bad or indifferent?"

"How did you guess that I had news?" inquired Miriam. Then without waiting for an answer she went on. "I certainly have, and very unpleasant news, at that."

"Out with it," said Nora, "and don't keep us in suspense."

"Well," said Miriam, "I suppose you all noticed how the juniors outwitted us at every point last Saturday? We put up a hard fight, too. The reason of it was that they knew every one of our signals."

"How dreadful!" "How did they get their information?" "Who told you so?" were the exclamations that rose from the assembled girls.

Grace had raised herself to a sitting position and was steadily regarding Miriam, who, well aware of that keen, searching gaze, deliberately continued:

"What makes the matter so much worse is the fact that we were betrayed by a member of our own class."

"Oh, Miriam, you don't mean that?" said Jessica.

"I am sorry to say that it is true," replied Miriam, "and I am going to put the matter before the class."

"Tell us who it is, Miriam," cried the girls. "We'll fix her!"

"Miriam," said Grace in a tone of quiet command that made every girl look toward her, "you are to mention no names while in my house."

Miriam's face flamed. Before she could reply, however, Grace went on. "Girls you must realize the position in which Miriam's remarks place me. She is sure that she knows who betrayed our signals, and is willing to name the person. Suppose she names some girl present. Think of the feelings of that girl, my guest, yet not safe from accusation while here. I should prove a poor sort of hostess if I allowed the honor of any of my friends to suffer while in my house.

"The place to discuss these things is in school. There every girl stands on an equal footing and can refute any charges made against her. I wish to say that I have a communication to make which may put a different face on the whole matter. I know something of the story of those signals. When I go back to school I shall call a meeting of the basketball team and its subs. and tell them what I know about it; but not until then. Furthermore it is not strictly a class matter, as it pertains to the basketball players alone. Therefore any one outside the team has no right to interfere. Please don't think me disagreeable. It is because I am trying to avoid unpleasant consequences that I am firm about having no names mentioned here."

There was an absolute silence in the room. The girls had a deep regard for Grace on account of her frank, open nature and love of fair play; but Miriam had her own particular friends who had respect for her on account of her being a Nesbit. She had a faculty of obtaining her own way, too, that seemed, to them, little short of marvellous, and she spent more money than any other girl in Oakdale High School. It was therefore difficult to choose between the two factions.

Nora broke the embarrassing pause.

"Grace is right as usual," she said, "and none of you girls should feel offended. What's the use of wasting the whole afternoon quarrelling over an old basketball game? Do talk about something pleasant. The sophomore ball for instance. Do you girls realize that we ought to be making some plans for it? It's the annual class dance, and should be welcomed, with enthusiasm. We've all been so crazy over basketball that we've neglected to think about our class responsibilities. We ought to try to make it a greater success than any other dance ever given by a sophomore class. We must call a meeting very soon, not to fight over basketball, but to make arrangements for our dance."

Nora's reminder of the coming ball was a stroke of diplomacy on her part.

What school girl does not grow enthusiastic over a class dance? A buzz of conversation immediately arose as to gowns, decorations, refreshments and the thousand and one things all important to a festivity of that kind.

Miriam seeing that it was useless to try to raise any further disturbance, cut her call short, taking with her several girls who were her staunch upholders.

Those who remained did not seem sorry at her departure, and Grace drew a breath of relief as the door closed upon the wilful girl. She had at least saved Anne from a cruel attack, but how much longer she could do so was a question. Miriam would undoubtedly bring up the subject at the first class meeting, and Grace was not so sure, now, that the girls would be willing to overlook the loss of the signals when she told them of it.

"I shall be loyal to Anne, no matter what it costs me," she decided. "She has done nothing wrong, and Miriam will find that she cannot trample upon either of us with impunity. As for Jessica and Nora, I know they will agree with me."

Under cover of conversation, Grace whispered to Jessica that she wished her to remain after the others had gone, and to ask Nora and Anne to do the same.

When the last of the callers had said good-bye, and the four chums had the room to themselves, Grace told Nora and Jessica about Anne's mishap, and how utterly innocent of blame she was.

"Do you mean to tell me that Miriam meant Anne when she said she could name the girl?" demanded Nora.

"She did, indeed," replied Anne, "and if it had not been for Grace she would have made things very unpleasant for me."

"Humph," ejaculated the fiery Nora, "then all I have to say is that I don't see how a nice boy like David ever happened to have a horrid hateful, scheming sister like Miriam. Stand up for Anne? Well I rather think so! Let Miriam dare to say anything like that to me."

"Or me," said Jessica.

"I knew you girls would feel the same as I do," said Grace. "Anne has some true friends, thank goodness. You see Miriam is basing all her suppositions on the fact that Anne was allowed to come to practice. She doesn't know anything about the loss of the signals. You remember she objected to Anne seeing the practice game. Now she will try to show that she was right in doing so."

"Let her try it," said Jessica, "She'll be sorry."

"I am not so sure of that," said Anne quietly. "You know that Miriam has plenty of influence with certain girls, while I am only a stranger about whom no one cares except yourselves and the boys and Mrs. Gray.

"You are the brightest girl in school just the same," said Nora, "and that counts for a whole lot. Miss Thompson likes you, too, and our crowd is not to be despised."

"You are the dearest people in the world," responded Anne gratefully. "Please don't think that I am unappreciative. You have done far too much for me, and I don't want you to get into trouble on my account. As long as you girls care for me, I don't mind what the others think."

"Don't say that Anne," said Jessica. "You don't know how mean some of those girls can be. Don't you remember the junior that was cut by her class last year? Of course, she did something for which she deserved to be cut, but the girls made her life miserable. The story went through every class, and she got the cold shoulder all around. She's not here this year. Her father sent her away to school, she was so unhappy. You remember her, don't you?" turning to Grace and Nora.

Both girls nodded. The story of the unfortunate junior loomed up before them. Every girl in High School knew it.

"We can only hope that history will not repeat itself," said Grace thoughtfully. "Of course, I don't mean that there is any similarity between the two cases. That girl last year was untruthful and extremely dishonorable. It is perfectly ridiculous to think of placing the blame for those signals upon Anne. If the girls are silly enough to listen to Miriam's insinuations, then they must choose between Miriam and me. Anne is my dear friend, and I shall stick to her until the end."

CHAPTER VIII

THE PRICE OF FRIENDSHIP

It was a week before Dr. Gale pronounced Grace fit to return to school. When she did make her appearance, she was hailed with delight by her schoolmates and made much of. Miss Thompson greeted her warmly. She was very fond of Grace, and had expressed great concern over the young girl's accident. It was unusual for a girl to receive so serious an injury during a game, as all rough play was strictly forbidden.

The principal had kept the members of both teams after school and questioned them closely. No one had seen Grace fall, nor realized that she was hurt until she had been discovered sitting on the gymnasium floor. Miss Thompson had a vague suspicion of foul play on the part of the juniors, but was unable to find out anything.

"Athletics for girls have always been encouraged in this school," she had said. "Rough play is disgraceful. If I found that any member of any High School basketball organization, either directly or indirectly, caused the injury of an opponent, I should forbid basketball for the rest of the season at least, and perhaps absolutely. Tripping, striking and kicking are barred out of the boys' games and will certainly not be tolerated in those of the girls."

As Grace was returning to the study hall from geometry recitation that morning, she encountered Julia Crosby. Julia glanced at her with an expression half fearful, half cunning, as though she wondered if Grace knew the truth about her fall.

Grace returned the look with one of such quiet contempt and scorn that Julia dropped her eyes and hurried along the corridor.

"How could she have been so contemptible?" thought Grace.

"I wonder if she'll tell," thought Julia. "She evidently knows I was responsible for her tumble. My, what a look she gave me. I wonder if that snippy little Anne Pierson knows about it, too. Very likely she does, for Grace Harlowe tells her all her business. If they do say anything I'll take good care no one believes it."

She was so absorbed in her own ruminations that she crashed into the dignified president of the senior class with considerable force, much to the glee of Nora, who happened to be near enough to catch the icy expression on the senior's face as Julia mumbled an apology.

At recess Grace notified the members of the basketball team and their substitutes that she had called a meeting to take place that afternoon at three o'clock in the sophomore locker room. "Only the basketball people are requested to be present," she concluded, "so don't bring any of the rest of the class."

At three o'clock precisely the last member had arrived. Every girl took particular pains to be there, for most of them had been at the Harlowe's on the day that Grace had silenced Miriam.

The meeting promised to be one of interest, for had not Grace Harlowe said that she would tell them something about the betrayed signals?

"Girls," Grace began, "you all know that although it is against the rules to allow any outsider to witness our practice, we have always made an exception in favor of Jessica. You all have perfect confidence in Jessica, I am sure. Since practice began this fall we have allowed Anne to come to it, too. You remember I asked permission for her to see the practice game, because I knew her to be absolutely trustworthy."

Here Nora nodded emphatically, Miriam tossed her head and smiled mockingly, while the rest of the girls looked a trifle mystified.

"Anne," continued Grace, "did not understand many of our plays, so I wrote out a list of signals for her, to study and learn by heart, telling her to destroy them as soon as she was sure she knew them. Unfortunately, she lost them, and at once told me about it. She felt very unhappy over it; but I told her not to worry, because I never supposed their loss would make any difference.

"When the game was well under way and the juniors began to block our plays, it flashed across me that in some way they had found that list. Anne, who has a mania for labeling everything, had written 'Sophomore basketball signals' across the paper; so, of course, any one who found it would know exactly what the list meant.

"We were warned that the juniors held a meeting at the Omnibus House a day or so before the game, and that they meant mischief. I never thought, however, they would be quite so dishonorable.

"I would have told you this before the game, but was afraid it would confuse and worry you. I am sure that you will agree with me, and absolve Anne from all blame."

"I don't agree with you at all," flashed Miriam, "and I am glad to have a chance to speak my mind. I told you before the game that I objected to Miss Pierson watching our practice, that it was against the rules, but no attention was paid to what I said. If you had taken my advice the result would have been far different. I have no doubt Grace believes that Miss Pierson lost the list, but I am not so easily deceived. I believe she deliberately handed it over to the juniors, and every loyal member of the team should cut her acquaintance."

"Miriam Nesbit," cried Nora. "You haven't the least right to accuse Anne Pierson of any such thing. She is too honorable to think of it, and she has no love for the junior class either. She isn't even friendly with them. If any one is to be accused of treachery, I should say that there are members of the team far more friendly with the juniors than poor little Anne."

This was a direct slap at Miriam, who winced a little at Nora's words.

"Well," said Marian Barber quickly, "it stands to reason that no member of the team would be foolish enough to help the enemy. I don't know anything about Miss Pierson, but I do know that I overheard Julia Crosby telling some girl in her class that the sophomores could thank one of their own class for their defeat."

"When did you hear her say that?" queried Miriam sharply.

"Yesterday morning. I was walking behind her, and she was so busy talking she didn't notice me."

"You girls can draw your own conclusions," said Miriam triumphantly. "That simply proves what I have said."

"That simply proves nothing at all," exclaimed Grace Harlowe, who had been too angry to trust herself to speak. "You are making a very serious charge against Anne without one bit of ground on which to base your suspicions. You have always disliked her because she won the freshman prize, and you know nothing whatever against her."

"No," said Miriam scornfully, "nor anything to her credit either. Who is she, anyway? The daughter of a strolling third-rate actor, who goes barnstorming about the country, and she has been on the stage, too. She has a very good opinion of herself since Mrs. Gray and certain Oakdale girls took her up, but I wouldn't trust her as far as I could see her. Why should girls of good Oakdale families be forced to associate with such people? I suppose she wanted to be on good terms with the juniors, too, and took that method of gaining her point."

"That is pure nonsense," exclaimed Nora. "Don't you think so, girls?"

But the other girls made no reply. They were thinking hard. Suspicion seemed to point in Anne's direction. What a pity Grace had been so rash about taking Anne up if her father were a common actor. Miriam was right about not caring to associate with Anne. After all, they knew very little about her. Grace Harlowe was always picking queer people and trying to help them.

"I think we ought to be very careful about taking outsiders into our confidence," firmly said Eva Allen, one of the team. "I didn't know Miss Pierson had ever been an actress." There was a note of horror in her voice as she pronounced the last word.

"I have always heard that they were very unreliable people," said another miss of sixteen.

Grace was in despair. She felt that she had lost. By dragging up Anne's unfortunate family history, Miriam had produced a bad impression that she was powerless to efface.

"Girls," she said, "you ought to be ashamed of yourselves. You know perfectly well that Anne is innocent. If you wish to be my friend you must be Anne's also. Please say that you believe her."

"Count on me," said Nora.

But the other sophomores had nothing to say.

Grace looked about her appealingly, only to meet cold looks and averted faces. Miriam was smiling openly.

"The meeting is adjourned," said Grace shortly, and without another word she went to her locker and began taking out her wraps. Nora followed her, but the majority of the girls walked over to the other end of the room and began to talk in low tones with Miriam.

Grace realized that her team had deserted her for Miriam. It was almost unbelievable. She set her lips and winked hard to keep back the tears which rose to her eyes. Then, followed by her one faithful friend, she walked out of the locker room, leaving her fickle classmates with their chosen leader.

CHAPTER IX

AN UNSUCCESSFUL INTERVIEW

There were two subjects of interest under discussion in the sophomore class. One was the coming ball, the other the story of the lost signals, which had gone the round of the class. The general opinion seemed to be that Anne had betrayed the team, and with the unthinking cruelty of youth, the girls had resolved to teach her a lesson. Miriam's accusation had been repeated from one girl to another, with unconscious additions, until Anne loomed up in the light of a traitor, and was treated accordingly.

Grace had told Anne the next day the details of the meeting, and in some measure prepared her for what would undoubtedly follow. Anne had laughed a little at the account of Miriam's remarks regarding her father, and the girls' evident disapproval of the theatrical profession.

"How silly they are," she said to Grace, who felt secretly relieved to know that Anne was not mortally hurt over Miriam's attack. "They don't know anything about professional people. Of course, there are plenty of worthless actors, but some of them are really very fine men and women. Miriam may abuse my family all she chooses, but I do feel unhappy to think that those girls believe me dishonorable and under-handed."

"They wouldn't if they had any sense," responded Grace hotly,

"I never believed that those girls could be so snobbish. I always thought them above such petty meanness. Don't pay any attention to them, Anne. They aren't worth it. I am going to interview Julia Crosby and make her acknowledge that she wasn't referring to you the other day. There is something queer about it all. I believe that there is some kind of secret understanding between Miriam and Julia; that this is a deliberate plot on their part to injure you and humiliate me, and I shall find out the truth before I am through."

"But what has Julia Crosby against me?" queried Anne, "I hardly know her."

"She hasn't forgotten the way David defended you at Mrs. Gray's Christmas ball last year," answered Grace, "Besides, you're a sophomore. Isn't that a good enough reason?"

"I suppose it is," said Anne wearily.

Grace kept her word and hailed Julia Crosby on the following afternoon as she was leaving the High School. It seemed a favorable opportunity for Julia was alone.

"Miss Crosby," said Grace coldly. "I should like to speak to you about a very important matter."

"There's nothing to hinder you, Miss Harlowe," replied Julia brusquely. "I'm here. Are you sure that it really is important?"

She stopped and eyed Grace insolently.

"I am very sure that it is important, Miss Crosby," said Grace. "Not long ago a certain sophomore overheard you telling a member of your class that we sophomores could thank a girl in our class for our basketball defeat. A certain girl had already been unjustly accused of betraying our signals. When your remark was repeated to the team, they immediately decided that you meant her. Since then her classmates have taken the matter up and are determined to cut her acquaintance."

"Well what has all this childish prattle to do with me?" demanded Julia rudely.

"It has this to do with you, that you can set the matter right by saying it was not Anne. You know perfectly well she had nothing to do with it. I don't know how you got those signals, but I do know that Anne never gave them to you."

"Did I say that she did?" asked Julia.

"No," said Grace, "neither did you say that she didn't."

"Very true," replied Julia in a disagreeable tone, "and I don't intend to say so either. She may or she may not have given them to me. I'll never tell. She's a snippy, conceited, little prig, and a little punishment for her sins will do her good."

"You are a cruel, heartless girl," cried Grace angrily. "Knowing Anne to be innocent, you refuse to clear her name of the suspicion resting upon it. Let me tell you one thing. I know who tripped me the day of the game, and so does Anne. If you don't clear Anne instantly, I shall go straight to Miss Thompson with it."

Grace's threat went home. Julia stood in actual dread of the principal. It looked as though the tables had been turned at last. If Grace went to Miss Thompson what a commotion there would be!

In a moment, however, Julia recovered herself. What was it Miss Thompson had said about rough play? Ah, Julia remembered now, and with the recollection of the principal's words came the means of worsting Grace Harlowe in her efforts to vindicate Anne.

"You may go to Miss Thompson if you think it wise," she said with a malicious smile, "but I wouldn't advise it - that is, unless you have gotten over caring for basketball."

"What do you mean?" asked Grace. Then like a flash she understood. If she should tell Miss Thompson the truth, the principal would believe her. Julia would receive her just deserts but, oh, bitter thought, there would be no more basketball that season.

Grace felt that she had no right to sacrifice the pleasure of so many others, even for Anne's sake. It would only increase the feeling against both Anne and herself, and after all, Julia might still hold out in her insinuations against Anne.

"How can you be so contemptible?" she said to her smiling enemy. "You never win anything honestly. I see it is useless for me to appeal to you for something which you cannot give, and that is fair play!" With a slight bow, Grace walked quickly away, leaving Julia a little astonished at her sudden departure and not at all pleased at Grace's frankly expressed opinion.

Grace lost no time in relating to Anne her fruitless interview with the junior captain.

"I am so humiliated to think I failed. I expected that threatening to tell Miss Thompson would bring her to her senses, but she is too cunning for me," sighed Grace.

The two girls were walking home from school.

"Shall you tell Nora and Jessica?" asked Anne.

"No," said Grace. "Let us keep the sprained ankle part of the story a secret. They are loyal to you, at any rate, and Nora would be so angry. I am afraid I couldn't keep her from going straight to Miss Thompson and making a general mess of things. I am so sorry, Anne, dear, but I guess we shall have to weather the gale together. It will die out after a while, just as all those things do. Hush! Don't say anything now. Here come Nora and Jessica."

"What do you think!" cried Nora. "Edna Wright is giving a

party next Saturday, and she isn't going to invite either you or Anne."

"How shocking!" said Grace. "We shall both die of grief at having been slighted."

She spoke lightly, and no one but Anne guessed how much the news hurt her.

"We are not going," declared Nora, "and we told her so."

"What did she say?" asked Grace.

"We didn't give her time to answer," said Nora, "but rushed off to find you. The whole thing is perfectly ridiculous! The idea of a lot of silly little school girls thinking they own the earth. It's all Miriam's fault. She has tried to be leader of her class ever since it was organized but mark what I say, she'll never accomplish it. Pride will get a fall, one of these days, and I hope I'll be around when it happens."

"Never mind, Nora," said Grace soothingly. "Anne and I don't care. We'll give a party at the same time, to our own crowd. I'll tell you what we'll do. We will have a surprise party for Mrs. Gray. I'll write to Tom Gray and ask him to come down for next Saturday. That will be a double surprise to dear Mrs. Gray."

"Fine!" cried Jessica. "We'll have Hippy and Reddy and David. Then our circle will be complete. The other crowd will be furious. Those boys are all popular, and I know that Edna intends to invite them."

"Let's tell them at once, then," said Nora, "before the other girls get a chance."

The boys were promptly invited. Grace sent a note to Tom Gray, who found it possible to get away for the week end.

Reddy, Hippy and David received invitations to the other party, but politely declined. Miriam endeavored to point out to her brother the folly of his conduct, but David simply stared at her and said nothing. He knew to what lengths her jealousy had carried her during the freshman year, and although Nora had entirely omitted his sister's name from the conversation when telling him of the recent trouble that had arisen, still David felt that Miriam was at the bottom of it.

Failing to elicit any response from her brother, she flew into a rage and did not speak to him for a week, while David went serenely on his way, and let her get over it as best she might.

The surprise party proved a success. Mrs. Gray's delight at seeing her "Christmas children" and having her beloved nephew with her was worth seeing. The young people did all the "stunts" they knew for her entertainment, and the boys repeated their Shakespearian performance for the old lady, who laughed until she could laugh no more.

It was their turn to be surprised, however, when the old butler suddenly appeared and announced that supper was served. Mrs. Gray had held a word of conversation with him directly after their arrival, which resulted in an array of good things calculated to tempt the appetite of any healthy boy or girl.

After supper they had an old-fashioned "sing," with Jessica at the piano, ending with "Home, Sweet Home" and the inevitable "Good Night, Ladies."

"I'm sure we had a better time than the other crowd," said Nora as they all walked down the street.

"Of course," said Grace, but a little feeling of sadness swept over her as she realized for the first time in her short life she had been slighted by any of her school friends.

CHAPTER X

THE SOPHOMORE BALL

It was the night of the sophomore ball. For a week past the class had been making preparations. The gymnasium had been transformed into a veritable bower of beauty. Every palm in Oakdale that could be begged, borrowed or rented was used for the occasion. Drawing rooms had been robbed of their prettiest sofa cushions and hangings, to make attractive cosy corners in the big room.

The walls were decorated with evergreens and class banners, while the class colors, red and gold, were everywhere in evidence. The sophomores had been recklessly extravagant in the matter of cut flowers, and bowls of red roses and carnations ornamented the various tables, loaned by fond mothers for the gratification of sophomore vanity.

The girls had worked hard to outdo previous sophomore affairs, and when all was finished the various teachers who were invited to view the general effect were unanimous in their admiration.

Once a year each of the four High School classes gave some sort of entertainment. Readers of "GRACE HARLOWE'S PLEBE YEAR" will remember the masquerade ball given by the sophomores, now juniors, and the active part taken by Grace and her chums in that festivity.

The present sophomores had decided to make their ball a larger affair than usual, and had sent out invitations to favored members of the other classes. An equal number of boys had been invited from the boys' High School, and the party promised to be one of the social events of Oakdale.

Mrs. Gray and a number of other prominent women of Oakdale, were to act as patronesses. Mrs. Harlowe, usually a favorite chaperon with Grace's crowd, had been ignored for the first time, and Grace was cut to the quick over it. As for Grace herself, she had not been appointed to a single committee. Prominent heretofore in every school enterprise, it was galling to the high-spirited girl to be deliberately left out of the preparations. Nora had been asked to help receive and Jessica had been appointed to the refreshment committee, but on finding that Grace was being snubbed, both had coldly declined to serve in either capacity.

The four chums held more than one anxious discussion as to the advisability of even attending the ball.

"I think we ought to go, just to show those girls that we are impervious to their petty insults," declared Grace. "We have as much right there as any one else, and I am sure the boys we know will dance with us whether the rest of the girls like it or not. Besides, Mrs. Gray will be there, and she will expect to see us. She doesn't know anything about this trouble, and I don't want her to know. It would only grieve her. She is so fond of Anne. By all means we must go to the ball. Wear your prettiest gowns and act as though nothing had happened."

That night, the four young girls, in their party finery, sat waiting in the Harlowe's drawing room for their escorts - David, Hippy and Reddy. Anne wore the pink crepe de chine which had done duty at Mrs. Gray's house party the previous winter. Grace wore an exquisite gown of pale blue silk made in a simple, girlish fashion that set her off to perfection. Nora was gowned in lavender and wore a corsage bouquet of violets that had mysteriously arrived that afternoon, and that everyone present suspected Hippy of sending. Jessica's gown was of white organdie, trimmed with tiny butterfly medallions and valenciennes lace.

In spite of the possibility that she and Anne might be the subject of unpleasant comment, Grace made up her mind to enjoy herself. She was fond of dancing, and knew that she would have plenty of invitations to do so. David would look after Anne, who was not yet proficient enough in dancing to venture to try it in public.

"If only Miriam and Julia Crosby behave themselves!" she thought, "for, of course, Julia will be there. Miriam will see that she gets an invitation."

Grace thrilled with pride as she entered the gymnasium. How beautifully it had been decorated and how well everything looked. She was so sorry that the girls had seen fit to leave her out of it all. Then she remembered her resolution to forget all differences and just have a good time.

Miriam, gowned in apricot messaline trimmed with silver, was in the receiving line with half a dozen other sophomores. Grace and her party would be obliged to exchange civilities with the enemy. She wondered what Miriam would do. David solved this problem for her by taking charge of the situation. Walking straight up to Miriam, he said a few words to her in a low tone. She flushed slightly, looked a trifle defiant then greeted the girls coldly, but with civility. The other sophomores followed her example, but Grace breathed a sigh of relief as they walked over to where Mrs. Gray, in a wonderful black satin gown, sat among the patronesses.

"My dear children, I am so glad to see all of you!" exclaimed the sprightly old lady. "How fine all my girls look. You are like a bouquet of flowers. Grace is a bluebell, Anne is a dear little clove pink, Nora is a whole bunch of violets and Jessica looks like a white narcissus."

"Where do we come in?" asked David, smiling at Mrs. Gray's pretty comparison.

"Allow me to answer that question," said Hippy. "You are like the tall and graceful burdock. Reddy resembles the common, but much-admired sheep sorrel, while I am like that tender little flower, the forget-me-not. Having once seen me, is it possible to forget me!" He struck an attitude and looked languishingly at Nora.

"I'll forget you forever if you look at me like that," threatened Nora.

"Never again," said Hippy hastily. "Bear witness, all of you, that my expression has changed."

Just then the first notes of the waltz "Amoreuse" rang out, and the gymnasium floor was soon filled with High School boys and girls dressed in their best party attire. The dances followed each other in rapid succession until supper was announced. This was served at small tables by the town caterer.

Mrs. Gray and her adopted children occupied two tables near together and had a merry time. Many curious glances were cast in their direction by the other members of the sophomore class.

Some of the girls wondered whether it was a good thing to cut Anne Pierson's acquaintance. She was certainly a friend of Mrs. Gray, and Mrs. Gray was one of the most influential women in Oakdale. Frances Fuller, a worldly-minded sophomore, dared to intimate as much to Miriam Nesbit, who replied loftily:

"If Mrs. Gray knew as much about Miss Pierson as we do, she would probably not care for her any longer."

"It's a pity some one doesn't tell her," said Julia Crosby, ever ready for mischief.

"Oh, some one will have the courage yet," answered Miriam, "and when she does, that will end everything as far as Miss Pierson is concerned. Mrs. Gray can't endure anything dishonorable."

Just then a young man claimed Miriam for the two-step about to begin, and Julia wandered off, leaving Frances to digest what had been said. The more the latter thought about it, the more she felt that Mrs. Gray ought to be warned against Anne. She decided that she had the courage; that it was her duty to do so.

Without hesitating, she blundered over to where Mrs. Gray sat for the moment.

"Mrs. Gray," Frances began, "I want to tell you something which I think you ought to know."

"And what is that, my dear?" asked the old lady courteously, trying vainly to remember the girl's face.

"Why, about Miss Pierson's true character," replied the girl.

"Miss Pierson's true character?" repeated Mrs. Gray. "I don't understand what you mean."

"That she is dishonorable and treacherous. She betrayed the sophomore basketball signals to the juniors, and then denied it, when her class had positive proof against her. Besides, her father is a disreputable actor, and she was an actress before she came here. We thought if you knew the truth you wouldn't uphold any such person." Frances paused. She thought she had made an impression upon her listener.

Mrs. Gray sat silent. She was too deeply incensed to trust herself to speak. Frances looked complacent. She evidently hoped to be commended for her plain speaking. Then Mrs. Gray found her voice.

"Young woman," she said, "you ought to be ashamed of yourself. What can you hope to gain by saying unkind things about a nice, gentle, little girl who is in every respect worthy of all the love and regard that can be given her? I do not know what you can be thinking of to speak so slightingly of one of your classmates, and I am sorry to be obliged to remind you that it is the height of ill breeding to abuse a person to his or her friends."

With these words, Mrs. Gray turned her back squarely upon the dazed girl, who slowly arose, and without looking at Mrs. Gray, walked dejectedly across the room. But Miriam Nesbit lost one supporter from that minute on.

"Hateful things," said the mortified Frances, looking towards Julia and Miriam. "I believe they are more to blame than Miss Pierson ever thought of being."

When Grace paused at Mrs. Gray's side after the two-step, she saw plainly that the old lady was much agitated.

"Grace," she said quickly, "what is all this nonsense about Anne?"

"O Mrs. Gray," cried Grace. "Who could have been so unkind as to tell you? We didn't want you to know. It is all so foolish."

"But I want to know," said the old lady positively. "Anne is so very dear to me, and I can't allow these hare-brained girls to make damaging statements about her. Tell me at once, Grace."

Grace reluctantly gave a brief account of her recent disagreement with her class and the unpleasantness to which Anne had been subjected.

"What does ail Miriam Nesbit? She used to be such a nice child!" exclaimed Mrs. Gray. "Really, Grace, I feel that I ought to go straight to Miss Thompson with this."

Grace's heart sank. That was just what she did not want Mrs. Gray to do.

"Dear Mrs. Gray," she said, patting the old lady's hand, "it is better for us to fight it out by ourselves. If Miss Thompson knew all that had happened, she would forbid basketball for the rest of the season. She is awfully opposed to anything of that kind, and would champion Anne's cause to the end, but Anne would rather let matters stand the way they are, than lose us our basketball privilege. You see, the juniors have won the first game, and if basketball were stopped now we would have no chance to make up our lost ground. I firmly believe that all will come right in the end, and I think the girls will get tired of their grudge and gradually drop it. Of course it hurts to be snubbed, but I guess we can stand it. We have some friends who are loyal, at any rate."

"I suppose you are right, my dear," responded the old lady. "It is better for old folks to keep their fingers out of young folk's pies. But what did that pert miss mean about Anne's father being an actor? I had an idea he was dead."

So Grace told Mrs. Gray the story of Anne's father, beginning from where he had intercepted Anne on her way from the aeroplane exhibition during her freshman year, up to the time of the arrival of his letter begging for money.

"Anne used her freshman prize money last year to help him out of trouble. He forged a friend's name for one hundred dollars, and would have had to go to prison had she not made good the money he took, I always wanted you to know about it, Mrs. Gray, but Anne felt so badly over it, she begged me never to tell any one."

"Your story explains a great many things I never before understood," said Mrs. Gray. "That doll that was sent to the Christmas party last year, for instance. But how did Miriam find out about it?"

"We don't know," said Grace. "Her doings are dark and mysterious. Find out she did; and she has told the story with considerable effect among the girls."

"It is too bad," mused Mrs. Gray. "I should like to right matters were it possible, but as long as you don't wish it, my dear, I suppose I must let you fight it out by yourselves. But one thing I am sure of, Anne shall never want for a friend as long as I live. Now run along and have a good time. I've kept you here when you might have been dancing."

"I have loved being with you," said Grace. "I shall not tell Anne about what was said," she added in a lower tone.

"That is right, Grace," responded Mrs. Gray. "No need of hurting the child's feelings."

During the balance of the evening nothing occurred to discomfit either Grace or Anne. To be sure there was a marked coolness exhibited by most of their classmates, but David took charge of Anne and saw to it that nothing disturbed her. Grace, who was a general favorite with the High School boys of Oakdale, could have filled her programme three times over. She was the embodiment of life and danced with such apparent unconcern that the mind of more than one sophomore was divided as to whether to cleave to Miriam or renew their former allegiance to Grace.

It was well after one o'clock when the "Home, Sweet Home" waltz sounded. The floor was well filled with dancers, for the majority of the guests had remained until the end of the ball. As the last strains of the music died away the sophomores sent their class yell echoing through the gymnasium. It was answered by the various yells of the other classes, given with true High School fervor. Each class trying to outdo the other in the making of noise.

Sleepy chaperons began gathering up their charges. The sophomore ball was a thing of the past.

"These late hours and indigestible suppers are bound to break down my delicate constitution yet," Hippy confided to Nora.

"In that case I shall make it a point to see that you don't receive any more invitations to our parties," Nora answered cruelly. "Then you can stay at home and build up that precious health of yours."

"Don't mention it," replied Hippy hastily. "I would rather become an emaciated wreck than deprive myself of your society."

"It was simply glorious," said Anne to Grace as they stood waiting for their carriage, "and was there ever such a nice boy as David!"

Grace pressed Anne's hand by way of answer. She knew that David had understood the situation and had taken care to steer Anne clear of shoals, and Grace determined that no matter what Miriam might say or do in future, for David's sake it should be overlooked.

CHAPTER XI

A LION AT LAST

It was a week before the last borrowed decoration reposed in its original place, and fully that long before the echoes of the sophomore ball died out. It was pronounced the most successful class function given in Oakdale for a number of years, and the sophomores felt justly proud of themselves. Miriam Nesbit took particular pains to point out that the success of the affair was in no way due to Grace Harlowe, and many of the girls who had hitherto believed that Grace was a necessary factor in High School fun, decided that they had perhaps overrated her ability.

Grace was fully cognizant of their change of heart, and spent more than one unhappy hour over it, but outwardly she carried herself as though unaware of the many little ill-natured stabs directed toward her. Anne, who was completely ignored, took it philosophically, her only regret being the fact that Grace had been dragged into difficulties on her account.

Thanksgiving had come and gone. The High School boys had played their usual game of football with a neighboring school and whipped them to a standstill, David had played on the team and covered himself with glory by making a sensational touchdown. The girl chums had worn his colors and shrieked themselves hoarse with joy over the prowess of their friend.

Miriam, secretly proud of her brother, resolved to make a like record for herself during the next basketball game, which was to take place during the following week. She believed that it was the last touch needed to make her the avowed leader of her class. She even dreamed that the basketball captaincy might one day be hers. To be sure Grace had Nora on her side, and Nora was one of the regular players, but the other two players were Miriam's faithful allies. That made three against two, and the second team had practically declared in her favor. Grace would have to do differently if she expected to keep the captaincy.

Meanwhile Grace was finding the captaincy of a team divided against itself anything but satisfactory. The girls, with the exception of Nora, obeyed her orders indifferently and as though under protest. It was almost impossible to get every member to come to practice. Some one of them invariably stayed away. On one occasion she spoke rather sharply to the team about it, but her earnest words were received with sullen resentment.

"What is the use of working ourselves to death simply to have our game handed over to the enemy?" one girl had muttered.

Grace colored at this thrust, but closed her lips tightly and made no reply. But the attitude of her team worked upon her mind, and she lost confidence in herself. She realized that a new and injurious influence was at work, and she was powerless to stem the tide of dissension that had arisen.

The practice game was played on the afternoon before the contest, and not even Jessica was there to witness it, although she had formerly been taken as a matter of course. When invited to attend practice she had scornfully refused it.

"No, thank you," she said. "If anything should go wrong tomorrow I'd be accused of treachery. No one's reputation is safe in this class." At which remark several sophomores had the grace to blush.

The day dawned bright and clear. Grace arrived at the gymnasium long before the others. She was worried and anxious over the behavior of her team. She was half afraid that some one of them would absent herself, in which case one of the substitutes would have to be called, and Grace doubted whether they could be relied upon.

Two months before, she had been certain that there were no players like those of the sophomore organization. Now she had no confidence in them or herself. She had a faint hope that when the game opened, her players would forget their grievances and work for the honor of the sophomores. She would do her best at all events, and Nora could be depended upon, too. All this passed rapidly through Grace's mind as she waited for the team to appear.

The spectators were arriving in numbers. The gallery was almost full, and it still lacked fifteen minutes of the time before the game would be called. The proverbial little bird had been extremely busy, and all sorts of rumors regarding the two teams were afloat. The juniors were, as usual, seated in a body and making a great deal of unnecessary noise. The members of the sophomore class were scattered here and there. Anne and Jessica sat with three or four of the girls who had refused to pay any attention to the talk about Anne. A dozen or more of Miriam's flock sat together watching for the appearance of their favorite. Occasionally they glanced over toward Anne, whispered to each other, and then giggled in a way that made Anne wince and Jessica feel like ordering them out of the gallery.

Grace and Nora stood talking together at one end of the gymnasium. Grace kept an anxious eye on the clock. It was five minutes of two and Miriam had not arrived. "Would she dare to stay away?" Grace wondered. At two minutes of two there was a burst of applause from the section of the gallery where Miriam's admirers were seated. Grace glanced quickly around to see what had caused it, and beheld Miriam serenely approaching, a satisfied smile on her face. She had waited until the last minute in the hope of making a sensation, and had not been disappointed. Then the game began.

Julia Crosby and Grace Harlowe once more faced each other on the field of action. This time Grace won the toss and sent the ball whizzing to the goal thrower, who tried for goal and caged the ball without effort. This aroused the sophomores, and Grace could have danced for joy as she saw that they were really going to work in earnest. The juniors were on the alert, too. If they won to-day that meant the season's championship. If they won the third game, that meant a complete whitewash for the sophomores.

So the juniors hotly contested every inch of the ground, and the sophomores found that they had their hands full. The first half of the game closed with the score 8 to 6 in favor of the juniors.

During the intermission of twenty minutes between halves, the sophomores retired to the little room off the gymnasium to rest. The outlook was indeed gloomy. It was doubtful whether they could make up their loss during the last half. Marian Barber, Eva Allen and Miriam whispered together in one corner. Grace sat with her chin in her hand, deep in thought, while Nora stood staring out the window trying to keep back the tears. Two or three of the substitutes strolled in and joined Miriam's group. The whispering grew to be a subdued murmur. The girls were evidently talking about Grace, hence their lowered voices. Their long-suffering captain looked at them once or twice, made a move as if to join them, then sat down again. Nora's blood was up at the girls' rudeness. She marched over to the group and was about to deliver her opinion of them in scathing terms, when the whistle sounded. There was a general scramble for places. Then the ball was put in play and the second half began.

The sophomores managed to tie the score during the early part of the last half, and from that on held their own. They fought strenuously to keep the juniors from scoring. When the juniors did score, the plucky sophomores managed to do the same soon after. There were two more minutes of the game, and the score stood 10 to 10. It looked as though it might end in a tie. One of the juniors had the ball. With unerring aim she threw it to goal. It never reached there, for Miriam Nesbit made a dash, sprang straight into the air and caught the ball before it reached its destination. Quick as a flash she threw it to Nora, who threw it to Marian Barber. The latter being near the basket threw it to goal without any trouble.

Before the juniors could get anywhere near the ball the whistle blew and the game closed. Score 12 to 10. The sophomores had won.

The noise in the gallery was deafening. Miriam's sensational playing had taken every one by storm. A crowd of sophomores rushed down to the gymnasium and began dancing around her singing their class song. Her cheeks were scarlet and her eyes blazed with triumph. She was a lion at last, and now the rest would follow. She felt sure that she would be asked to take the place of Grace as captain. She had shown them what she could do. Grace had done nothing but cause trouble. The team would be better off without her.

Anne and Jessica were waiting in the corridor for Grace and Nora. The two players rapidly changed their clothes and soon the chums were walking down the quiet street.

"Well," said Jessica, "Miriam has done it at last."

"She has, indeed," responded Grace, "and no one begrudges her her glory. She made a star play and saved the day for us. She is loyal to the team even if she doesn't like their captain."

"I don't know about that," said Nora, "I think she might have exerted herself during the first game if she wanted so much to show her loyalty. She was anything but a star player, then. I have no faith in her, whatever. She cares for no one but herself, and that star play was for her own benefit, not because of any allegiance to her team. She's up to something, you may depend upon that."

"Oh, Nora, don't be too hard on her. She deserves great credit for her work. Don't you think so, girls?" Grace turned appealingly to Anne and Jessica.

"It was a remarkable play," said Anne.

Jessica made no answer. She would not praise Grace's enemy, even to please Grace.

"You may say what you please," said Nora obstinately, "I shall stick to my own convictions. The way those girls stood in the corner and whispered during intermission was simply disgraceful. Mark my words, something will come of it."

"Oh, here comes David on his motorcycle," called Anne delightedly.

David slowed up when he saw the girls, alighted and greeted them warmly. He at once congratulated them on their victory.

"I congratulate you on having a star player for a sister," said Grace. "It must run in the family." She referred to his late football triumphs.

David flushed with pleasure, more at the compliment paid to his sister than the one meant for him.

"Sis can come up to the mark when she wants to," he said earnestly. "I hope she repeats the performance." Then he abruptly changed the subject. That one little speech revealed to his friends the fact that he understood the situation and longed with all his heart for a change of tactics on the part of his sister.

CHAPTER XII

THE WAYS OF SCHOOLGIRLS

The clang of the gong announced the end of school for the day, but some of the sophomores lingered in their locker-room.

They had a very disagreeable communication to make that afternoon, to one of their class, and now that the time had come were inclined to shrink from the ordeal.

"I think Miriam should break the news herself," observed Marian Barber, "as long as she is to succeed Grace."

"Miriam isn't here," said Eva Allen, "she went home early. She told me she could not bear to see anyone unhappy. She is so sensitive you know?" Eva Allen was devoted to Miriam's cause.

"Oh, I don't know about that," said practical Marian. "She'll make a good captain, however, because she has showed more loyalty to the team than Grace has."

Marian firmly believed what she said. She had never been an ardent admirer of Miriam, and had at first stubbornly refused to repudiate Grace. But Miriam had little by little instilled into her the idea of Grace's incompetency, until Marian, who thought only of the good of the team, became convinced that a change of captains was advisable. Miriam's brilliant playing in the recent game was the final touch needed, and now Marian was prepared to do what she considered was her absolute duty.

"Suppose we write Grace a letter," suggested one of the substitutes, "as long as no one seems anxious to tell her."

"Hush," exclaimed Eva Allen, holding up her finger. "Here come Nora and Jessica. I know they are going to make a lot of fuss when they hear the news. Suppose we go back to the classroom and write the letter. We can all sign our names to it, and then we'll be equally to blame."

The conspirators accordingly trooped into the corridor, just as Nora and Jessica were about to enter the locker-room.

"What in the world is the matter now?" called Jessica. "You girls looks as guilty as though you'd stolen a gold mine."

"Wait and see," said Eva with a rather embarrassed laugh, as she hurried after the others up the stairs.

"Do you know, Jessica, I believe they're up to some hateful mischief. What did I tell you the other day? Those girls have given Grace the cold shoulder more than ever, since the game. They have been following Miriam about like a lot of sheep. Grace notices it, too, and it makes her unhappy, only she's too proud to say so."

"Never mind," said Jessica soothingly. "They'll be sorry some day. Miriam's influence won't last. Grace did perfectly right in standing by Anne, and you and I must always stand by Grace. Grace is a fine captain, and -"

"What are you saying about me?" demanded Grace herself, walking into the locker-room with Anne.

Jessica blushed and was silent, but Nora said glibly, "Oh, Jessica just now said that you made a fine captain." Then she went on hurriedly, "I think our chances for winning the championship are better than ever, don't you?"

"The juniors have been practising like mad since their defeat," mused Grace. "They will make a hard fight next time. Miss Thompson told me yesterday that she never saw better work in basketball than ours last Saturday. I am so proud of my team, even though they haven't been very nice to me lately. My whole desire is for them to win the final game. I suppose a captain has about the same feeling toward her players that a mother has toward her daughters. She is willing to make any sacrifice in order to make fine girls of them."

"And you are a fine captain," cried Anne. "I felt so proud of you the other day. You handled your team so well. Knowing how hateful they have been, it was wonderful to see you give your orders as though nothing had happened. No other girl could have done it."

"That is a nice compliment, Anne, dear," said Grace pleased with the words of praise from her friend, for the bitterness of her recent unpopularity had made her heart heavy.

At that moment the sophomores whom Jessica and Nora had encountered filed into the room.

Each girl wore a self-conscious expression. Eva Allen carried an envelope in her hand. She was confused and nervous.

Once inside the door the girls paused and began a whispered conversation. Then Eva Allen tried to push the envelope into another girl's hand; but the girl put her hands behind her back and obstinately refused to take it. There was another whispered conference with many side glances in Grace's direction.

Nora stood scowling savagely at the group. She noticed that it consisted of the basketball team and its substitutes. They were all there except Miriam.

"If you have any secrets, girls," remarked Grace in a hurt tone, "please postpone the telling of them for a few minutes. I am going, directly."

She opened her locker and drew out her coat and hat, trying to hide the tears that filled her eyes.

Then Marian Barber impatiently took the envelope from Eva and stepped forward. She had made up her mind to get the whole thing over as rapidly as she could.

"Er - Grace," she said, clearing her throat, "er - the team has -"

"Well, what is it?" exclaimed Nora, irritated beyond her power of endurance. "Why don't you speak out, instead of stuttering in that fashion? I always did detest stuttering."

"Marian has a note for you, Grace," interposed one of the substitutes growing bolder.

Marian placed the note in Grace's hand and turned slowly away. Up to that minute she had believed that what they were about to do was for the best; but all at once the feeling swept over her that she had done a contemptible thing. She turned as though about to take the envelope from Grace, but the latter had already opened it, and unfolding the paper began reading the contents aloud.

"Dear Grace," she read, "after a meeting to-day of the members of the regular and substitute sophomore basketball teams, it was decided that your resignation as captain of the same be requested.

"We are sorry to do this, but we believe it is for the good of the team. We feel that you cannot be loyal to its interests as long as you persist in being a friend of one of its enemies."

The names of the players, with the exception of Nora's and Miriam's, were signed to this communication.

After she had finished reading Grace stood perfectly still, looking searchingly into the faces of her classmates. She was trying to gain her self-control before speaking to them.

She could hardly realize that her own team had dealt this cruel blow. For the first time in her life she had received a real shock. She took a long deep breath and clenched her hands. She did not wish to break down before she had spoken what was in her mind.

Nora was muttering angrily to herself. Jessica looked ready to cry, while Anne, pale and resolute, came over and stood by Grace. She felt that she had been the primary cause of the whole trouble. She had borne the girls' unjust treatment of herself in silence, but, now, they had visited their displeasure upon Grace, and that was not to be borne.

"How dared you do such a despicable thing?" she cried. "You are cruel, unfeeling, and oh, so unjust. You accused me of something I would scorn to do, and not satisfied with that, visited your petty spite upon a girl who is the soul of truth and honor. You may say what you choose about me, but you shall not hurt Grace, and if you don't immediately retract what you have written I will take measures which may prove most unpleasant to all of you."

Just what Anne intended to do she did not know, but her outburst had its effect on the conspirators, and they squirmed uneasily under the lash of her words. Perhaps, they had misjudged this slender, dark-eyed girl after all.

Before Anne could say more, Grace spoke quietly.

"Sit down, all of you," she said at last, with a sweetness and dignity that was remarkable in so young a girl. "I have something to say to you. It is curious," she went on, "that I was just talking about our basketball team when you came into the room. I had said to Nora, Jessica and Anne that I wanted more than anything else in the world to beat the junior team. Miss Thompson had been praising the team to me, and I said to the girls that I thought I loved it just as a mother loves her daughters. There is no sacrifice I wouldn't make to keep up the team's good work, and that is the reason why I am going to make a sacrifice, now, and decline to resign. If I had been a poor captain, you would have had a right to ask for my resignation But I haven't. I have been a good, hard-working, conscientious captain, and I have made a success of the team. None of you can deny it. If you took a new captain at this stage it might ruin everything, and I tell you I have thought too much about it; I have set my heart on it so firmly that it would just break if we lost the deciding game."

Her voice broke a little. Nora was sobbing openly. It was hard work for Grace to control her own tears.

"Of course," she went on, clearing her throat and raising her voice to steady it, "it will be a sacrifice for me to keep on being your captain when you don't want me. It's no fun, I can assure you. Perhaps none of you has ever felt the hurt that comes of being turned out by people who were once fond of you. I hope you never will. I am still fond of all of you, and some day, perhaps, you will see that you have made a mistake. At any rate, I decline to resign my place. It was given to me for the year, and I won't give it up."

Grace turned her back and walked to the window. She had come at last to the end of her strength. She leaned against the window jamb and wept bitterly.

But the address of Mark Anthony over the dead body of Caesar was not more effective than this simple schoolgirl's speech. Every girl there melted into tears of remorse and sympathy.

"Oh, Grace," cried Marian Barber, "won't you forgive us? We never dreamed it would hurt you so. Now that I look back upon it, I can't see how we could have asked you to do it. We did believe that Miss Pierson betrayed us; but after all, that had nothing to do with your being captain of the team. I think you have been a great deal more loyal than we have. I want to say right here, girls, that I apologize to Grace and scratch my name off the list."

She took a pencil, dashing it through her signature, which was the first one on the letter.

One by one each of the other girls put a pencil stroke through her name.

Then they pinned on their hats, slipped into their coats and left the room as quickly as possible. They were all desperately ashamed; each in her secret heart wished she had never entered into the conspiracy.

They had given the captaincy to Grace, and after all, they had no right to take away what they had freely given, and for no better reason than that Grace was loyal to a friend whom they distrusted.

It was a cruel thing that they had done. They admitted it to each other now, and wished they had never listened to Miriam Nesbit.

Speaking of Miriam, who was to tell her that she had not supplanted Grace after all, as captain of the team.

"You are all cowards," exclaimed Marian Barber still buoyed up by her recent emotions, "I am not afraid of Miriam, or anyone else, and I'll undertake to tell her."

But at the last moment she determined to break the news by letter.

In the meantime, Miss Thompson had quietly entered the locker-room, where Grace and her three chums were still standing.

"Grace," said the principal, "I was passing by and I could not help overhearing what has been said, and while I don't care to enter into the little private quarrels of my girls, I want to tell you that you made a noble defense of your position. I am very proud of you, my child." Miss Thompson put her arms around the weeping girl and kissed her. "I wish every girl in my school would make such a stand for her principles. You were right not to have resigned. Always do what your judgment tells you is right, no matter what the result is, and don't give up the captaincy!"

CHAPTER XIII

A SKATING PARTY

The holidays had come and gone, and the pupils of Oakdale High School had resigned themselves to a period of hard study. The dreaded mid-year examinations stared them in the face, and for the time being basketball ardor had cooled and a surprising devotion to study had ensued.

Since the day that Grace had refused to give up her captaincy there had been considerable change in the girls' attitude toward her. She had not regained her old-time popularity, but it was evident that her schoolmates respected her for her brave decision and treated her with courtesy. They still retained a feeling of suspicion toward Anne, however, although they did not openly manifest it.

Miriam Nesbit had been inwardly furious over the outcome of her plan to gain the captaincy, but she was wise enough to assume an air of indifference over her defeat. Grace's speech had made considerable impression on the minds of even Miriam's most devoted supporters and she knew that the slightest slip on her part would turn the tide of opinion against her.

Grace was in a more cheerful frame of mind than formerly. She felt that all would come right some day. "Truth crushed to earth shall rise again," she told herself, and the familiar saying proved very comforting to her.

Winter had settled down on Oakdale as only a northern winter can do. There had been snow on the ground since Thanksgiving, and sleigh rides and skating parties were in order.

Grace awoke one Saturday morning in high good humor.

"To-day's the day," she said to herself. "Hurrah for skating!"

She hurried through her breakfast and was donning her fur cap and sweater, when Anne, Jessica and Nora, accompanied by David, Hippy, Reddy and, to her surprise and delight, Tom Gray, turned in at her gate.

"'Oh, be joyful, oh, be gay,
For there's skating on the bay,'"

sang Hippy.

"Meaning pond, I suppose," laughed Grace, as she opened her front door.

"Meaning pond?" answered Hippy, "only pond doesn't rhyme with gay."

"You might say,

"'Oh, be joyful, oh, be fond,
For there's skating on the pond,'"

suggested David.

"Fond of what?" demanded Hippy.

"Of the person you've asked to skate with you," replied David, looking toward Anne, who stood with a small pair of new skates tucked under her arm.

"I shall be initiated into all the mysteries of the world soon," she observed, smiling happily. "Last year it was coasting and football and now it's dancing and skating. When I once get these things on, David, I'll be like a bird trying its wings, I'll flop about just as helplessly."

"I'm awfully glad to see you, Tom," said Grace, "I did not expect to see you until Easter."

"Oh, I couldn't keep away," laughed Tom. "This is the jolliest place I know."

"Good reason," said Reddy, "we are the real people."

"Stop praising yourself and listen to me," said Hippy. "Our pond has frozen over in the most obliging manner. It's as smooth as glass. Let's go there to skate. There's a crowd of boys and girls on it already."

The pond on the Wingate estate was really a small lake, a mile or more in circumference. While it froze over every winter, the ice was apt to be rough, and there were often dangerous places in it, air-holes and thin spots where several serious accidents had occurred.

Therefore, Wingate's Pond was not used as much as the river for skating; but this winter the ice was as smooth and solid as if it had been frozen artificially, so the High School boys and girls could not resist the temptation to skim over its surface.

"Isn't it a fine sight?" asked Grace, as they came in view of the skaters who were circling and gliding over the pond, some by twos and threes, others in long rows, laughing and shouting.

A big fire burned on the bank, rows of new-comers sat near it, fitting on their skates.

"Away with dull care!" cried Hippy, as he circled gracefully over the ice; for, with all his weight, Hippy was considered one of the best skaters in Oakdale.

"Away with everything but fun," finished Grace who could think of nothing save the joy of skating. "Come along, Anne. Don't be afraid. David and I will keep you up until you learn to use those tiny little feet of yours."

Anne's small feet went almost higher than her head while Grace was speaking, and she sat flat down on the ice.

"No harm done," she laughed, "only I didn't know it could possibly be so slippery."

They pulled her up, David and Grace, and put her between them with Tom Gray on the other side of Grace as additional support, and off they flew, while Anne, keeping her feet together and holding on tightly, sailed along like a small ice boat.

"This will give you confidence," explained David, "and later on you can learn how to use your feet."

But Anne hardly heard him, so thrilled was she by the glorious sensation. As they flew by, followed by Hippy and Nora, with Reddy and Jessica, she caught glimpses of many people looking strangely unfamiliar on skates. Miriam passed, gliding gracefully over the ice with a troop of sophomores at her heels. There were many High School boys "cracking the whip" in long rows of eight or more, while there were some older people comfortably seated in sleigh chairs which were pushed from behind, generally by some poor boys in Oakdale, who stood on the bank waiting to be hired.

"Now, we'll have a lesson," exclaimed David when they had reached the starting point again, while the others lost themselves in the crowd. Anne was a good pupil, but she was soon tired and sat down on a bench near the bank.

"Do go and have a good skate yourself, David," she insisted. "I'll rest for awhile and look on."

Jessie Graham Flower

But it was far too cold to sit still.

"I'll give myself a lesson," she said. "This is a quiet spot. All the others seem to have skated up to the other end."

As she was carefully taking the strokes David had taught her, with an occasional struggle to keep her balance, she heard a great shouting behind her. The next instant, some one had seized her by the hand.

"Keep your feet together!" was shouted in her ear, and she found herself going like the wind at the end of a long line of girls. They were juniors, she saw at once, and it was Julia Crosby at the whip end who had seized her by the hand.

Anne closed her eyes. They were going at a tremendous rate of speed, it seemed to her, like a comet shooting through the air. Then, suddenly, the head of the comet stood still and the tail swung around it, and Anne, who represented the very tip of the tail and who hardly reached to Julia Crosby's shoulder, felt herself carried along with such velocity that the breath left her body, her knees gave way and she fell down in a limp little bundle. Julia Crosby instantly let go her hand and the impetus of the rush shot her like a catapult far over the ice into the midst of a crowd of skaters.

But the juniors never stopped to see what damage had been done. They quickly joined hands again, and were off on another expedition almost before Anne had been picked up by David and Hippy.

"It's that Julia Crosby again," cried David. "I wish she would move to Europe. I'd gladly buy her a ticket. The town of Oakdale isn't big enough to hold her and other people. She's always trying to knock somebody off the side of the earth."

Anne went home, tired and bruised. She had had enough of skating for one morning David returned to join the others; for this was not the last of the day's adventures and Julia Crosby, before sunset, was to repent of her cruelty to Anne.

In the meantime Grace and Tom had skated up to the far end of the pond.

"Well, Grace," said Tom, "how has the world been using you? I suppose you have been adding to your laurels as a basketball captain."

"Far from it," said Grace a trifle sadly. "Miriam Nesbit is star player at present."

They skated on for some time in silence. Tom felt there was something wrong, so he tactfully changed the subject.

"Who is the girl doing the fancy strokes?" he asked, pointing to Julia Crosby, who, some distance ahead of them, was giving an exhibition of her powers as a maker of figure eights and cross-cuts.

"That's the junior captain," answered Grace. "I hope she won't fall, because she's heavy enough to go right through the ice if she should have a hard tumble."

"Suppose we stop watching her," suggested Tom. "I don't want to see her take a header, and people who show off on skates always do so, sooner or later."

They changed their course toward the middle of the pond, while Julia, who was turning and circling nearer the shore, watched them from one corner of her eye.

Suddenly Grace stopped.

"Julia! Julia!" she cried. "Miss Crosby!"

"What's the matter?" demanded Tom.

"Don't you see the danger flag over there? She will skate into a hole if she keeps on. The ice houses are near here, and I suppose it is where they have been cutting ice."

"Hello-o!" cried Tom, straining his lungs to reach the skater, who looked back, gave her usual tantalizing laugh and skated on.

"You are getting onto thin ice," screamed Grace in despair, beckoning wildly. "Stop! Stop!"

Julia Crosby was skating backwards now, facing the others.

"Catch me if you can," she called, and the wind carried her words to them as they flew after her.

Then Grace, who had been anxiously watching the skater and not the ice, stumbled on a piece of frozen wood and fell headlong. She lay still for an instant, half stunned by the blow, but even in that distressful moment she could hear the other girl's derisive laughter.

Tom called again:

"You'll be drowned, if you don't look where you are going."

"Why don't you learn to skate?" was Julia's answer.

"O Tom," exclaimed Grace. "Leave me. I'll soon get my breath. Do go and stop that girl. The pond's awfully deep there."

"Miss Crosby," Tom Gray called, "won't you wait a minute? I have something to tell you."

"Catch me first!" she cried.

She turned and began skating for dear life, bending from the waist and going like the wind.

"I think I'll try and catch her from the front," he said to himself. "I don't propose to tumble in, too, and leave poor Grace to fish, us both out."

With arms swinging freely, he made for the center of the pond. As he whizzed past the girl, he turned with a wide sweep and came toward her, pointing at the same time to the white flag. But it was too late. In her effort to outstrip him, Julia slid heavily into the danger zone.

There was a crash and a splash, then down she went into the icy water, followed by Tom, who had seized her arm in a fruitless effort to save her.

For an instant Tom was paralyzed with the coldness of the water. Still, keeping a firm grip on the arm of the girl who had been responsible for his ice bath, he managed to clutch the ledge of ice made by their fall with his free hand.

"Take hold of the ice and try to help yourself a little," commanded Tom.

Julia made a half-hearted attempt, and managed to grasp the ledge, but her hold was so feeble that Tom dared not withdraw his support He was powerless to act, and they would both drown unless help came quickly.

CHAPTER XIV

A BRAVE RESCUE

Grace was still where she had fallen, cooling a large, red lump on her forehead by applying her handkerchief first to the ice and then to the swollen place, when she suddenly felt herself to be entirely alone in the world.

"Everybody has gone home to dinner!" she exclaimed, as she glanced over her shoulder at the other end of the pond, now denuded of skaters.

Then she shifted her position, looking for Tom and Julia. She had never dreamed, when she saw her friend go whizzing across the ice, that he had not caught the reckless girl in time to warn her of her danger.

In a flash she saw the empty expanse of ice before her. She leaped to her feet, balancing herself with difficulty, for her head was still dizzy from the blow.

"Tom! Tom Gray!" she called. "Where are you?"

"Run for help!" came the answer. In another moment she saw them clinging to a broken ledge of ice, Tom supporting Julia Crosby.

As for the junior captain, she was weeping bitterly, and making no attempt to help herself.

Grace anxiously scanned the expanse of the ice. It was nearly a mile to the other end of the pond, and the last group of skaters had disappeared over the brow of the hill.

"You must think quickly," she said to herself.

Her eyes took in the other shore. Not a soul was there, not a dwelling of any sort; nothing but the great ice house that stood like a lonely sentinel on the bank. Yet something seemed to tell her that help lay in that direction.

Once before, in a moment of danger, Grace had obeyed this same impulse and had never regretted it. Once again she was following the instinct that might have seemed to another person anything but wise.

Skating as she had never skated before, Grace Harlowe reached the shore in a moment. Here, dropping to the bank, she quickly removed her skates, then ran toward the ice house, feeling strangely unaccustomed to walking on the ground after her long morning on skates.

"What if I am off on a wild-goose chase?" she said to herself. "Suppose there is no one there?" She paused for an instant and then ran on faster than before.

"I shall find help over there, I know I shall," she thought as she hurried over the frozen ground and made straight for the ice house. There was no time to be lost. Tom and Julia were liable to be sucked under and drowned while she was looking for help.

Grace pushed resolutely on. In the meantime hardly four minutes had really elapsed since the skaters had tumbled into the water.

On the other side of the ice house she came abruptly upon a man engaged in loading a child's wagon with chips of wood.

Jessie Graham Flower

"Help!" cried Grace. "Help! Some people have broken through the ice. Have you a rope?"

The man made no answer whatever. He did not even look up until Grace shook him by the shoulder.

"There is no time to lose," she cried. "They may drown at any moment. Come! Come quickly, and help me save them."

The man looked at her with a strange, far-away expression in his eyes.

"Don't you hear me?" cried Grace in an agony of impatience. "Are you deaf?"

He shook his head stupidly, touching his ears and mouth.

"Deaf and dumb!" she exclaimed in despair.

Holding up two fingers, Grace pointed toward the water. Then she made a swimming motion. Perhaps he had understood. She could not tell, but her quick eye had caught sight of a long, thin plank on the shore.

Pulling off one of her mittens, she showed him a little pearl and turquoise ring her mother had given her for a birthday present, indicating that she would give it to him if he would help her. Then she seized one end of the plank and made a sign for him to take the other; but the stubborn creature began to unload the chips from the wagon.

Grace ran blindly ahead, dragging the plank alone.

"He's feeble-minded," she quivered. "I suppose I shall have to work this thing by myself."

When she had reached the bank, Grace heard him trotting behind her with his little wagon. In another moment there was a tug at the board. She turned and shook her fist angrily at him; but, without regarding her in the least, he lifted the plank and rested it on the wagon. Then motioning her to hold up the back end, he started on a run down the bank.

"The poor soul thinks he's a horse, I suppose," she said to herself, "but what difference does it make, if we can only get the plank to Tom and Julia?"

Grace soon saw, however, that the idea was not entirely idiotic. Later she was to offer up a prayer of thanks for that same child's wagon. The deaf and dumb man was wearing heavy Arctic rubbers, which kept him from slipping; while Grace, whose soles were as smooth as glass, kept her balance admirably by means of the other end of the plank.

Tom and Julia Crosby had now been nearly ten minutes in the water. Twice the ice had broken under Tom's grasp, while Julia, who seemed unable to help herself, had thrown all her weight on the poor boy, while she called wildly for help and heaped Grace with reproaches for running away.

"If it were not for the fact that it would be the act of a coward," exclaimed Tom at last, his teeth chattering with cold, "I would let go of your arm and give up the job of supporting you in this ice water for talking about Grace like that. Of course she has gone for help. Haven't you found out long ago that she is the right sort?"

"Well, why did she go in the wrong direction?" sobbed Julia. "Everybody is over on the other bank. There is nothing but an ice house over here."

"You may trust to her to have had some good, sensible reason," retorted Tom loyally.

"I don't think I can keep up much longer," exclaimed Julia, beginning to cry again.

"Keep on crying," replied Tom exasperated. "It will warm you

- and remember that I am doing the keeping up. I don't see that you are making any special effort in that direction."

Once Tom had endeavored to lift Julia out of the hole, and he believed, and always insisted, in telling the story afterwards, that if she had been willing to help herself it could have been accomplished. But Julia Crosby, triumphant leader of her class, and Julia Crosby cold and wet as a result of her own recklessness, were two different beings altogether.

"Grace Harlowe has left us to drown," she sobbed. "I am so wretched. She is a selfish girl."

"No such thing," replied Tom vigorously. "Here she comes now, bringing help as I expected I should think you'd be ashamed of yourself." He gave a sigh of relief when he saw Grace and the strange man approaching at a quick trot, the wagon and plank between them. His confidence in Grace had not been misplaced. He felt that they would soon be released from their perilous predicament.

"All right," called Grace cheerfully as she approached. "Keep up a little while longer. We'll have you both out in a jiffy."

Both rescuers slid the plank on the ice until one end projected over the hole.

Then the man and Grace both lay flat down on the other end and Grace called "ready."

Julia Crosby seized the board and pulled herself out of the water, safe, now, from the breaking of thin ice at the edge.

"Now, Tom," cried Grace.

But Julia's considerable weight had already weakened the wood. When Tom attempted to draw himself up, crack! went the board, and a jagged piece broke off. This would not have been so serious if the ice had not given way. Then, into the water, with many strange, guttural cries, slipped the deaf and dumb man. Grace herself was wet through by the rush of water over the ice, and just saved herself by slipping backward.

There was still a small portion of the plank left, and, with Julia Crosby's help, Grace thought they might manage to pull the two men out.

But Julia looked hardly able to help herself. She sat shivering on the bank trying to remove her skates.

"Julia," called Grace desperately. "You must help me now or these two men will drown. Help me hold down this plank."

Aroused by Grace's appeal, Julia meekly obeyed, and, still shivering violently, knelt beside Grace on the plank. But it was too short; when Tom Gray seized one end of it he nearly upset both the girls into the water.

"Oh, what shall we do?" cried Grace in despair when suddenly there came the thought of the little wagon.

Quickly untwisting a long muffler of red silk from about her neck, Grace tied it securely in the middle, around the cross piece of the tongue of the stout little vehicle. Then she pushed it gently until it stood on the edge of the hole. Giving one end of the muffler to Julia, Grace took the other herself.

"Catch hold of the tail piece, Tom," she cried.

Fortunately the ice was very rough where the girls were standing, or they would certainly have slipped and fallen. They pulled and tugged until gradually the ice in front of them, with Tom's additional weight on it, instead of breaking began to sink. But Tom Gray was out of the hole now; helped by the wagon he slipped easily along the half-submerged ice, then finally rolled over with a cry of relief upon the firm surface.

In the same way they pulled out the deaf and dumb man, who

had certainly been brave and patient during the ordeal, although he had uttered the most fearful sounds.

As soon as his feet touched the solid ice, he seized his wagon and made for the bank. Grace, remembering she had promised him her ring, hurried after him, but she was chilled to the bone and could not run. By the time she reached the bank he had rounded the corner of the ice house and was out of sight.

"He evidently doesn't care to be thanked," said Tom Gray as Grace returned to where he and Julia stood waiting.

"We had better get home as soon as possible or we'll all be laid up with colds."

The three half-frozen young people made their way home as best they could. Their clothes had frozen stiff, making it impossible for them to hurry. Julia Crosby said not a word during the walk, but when she left them at the corner where she turned into her own street, she said huskily: "Thank you both for what you did for me to-day, I owe my life to you."

"That was a whole lot for her to say," said Grace.

"She ought to be grateful," growled Tom. "She was the cause of all this mess," pointing to his wet clothes.

"I believe she will be," said Grace softly, "After all, 'It's an ill wind that blows no one good.'"

Grace's mother was justly horrified when Grace, in her bedraggled condition, walked into the living room. She insisted on putting her to bed, wrapping her in blankets and giving her hot drinks. Grace fell into a sound sleep from which she did not awaken until evening. Then she rose, dressed and appeared at the supper table apparently none the worse for her wetting.

Meanwhile Tom Gray had gone to his aunt's, given himself a

brisk rubbing down and changed his wet clothing for another suit he fortunately happened to have with him. Thanks to his strong constitution and vigorous health, he felt no bad effects.

He then went down to the kitchen, asked the cook for a cup of hot coffee, and, after hastily swallowing it, rushed off to find David, Hippy and Reddy and tell them the news. He was filled with admiration for Grace.

"She is the finest, most resolute girl I ever knew!" he exclaimed as he finished his story.

"Hurrah for Grace Harlowe!" shouted Reddy.

"Let's go down to-night and see if she's all right?" suggested David.

Before seven o'clock the four boys were on their way to the Harlowe's. They crept quietly up to the living-room window. Grace sat by the fire reading. Very softly they began a popular song that was a favorite of hers. Grace's quick ears caught the sound of the music. She was out of the house like a flash, and five minutes later the four boys were seated around the fire going over the day's adventure.

"The deaf and dumb man who helped you out is quite a character," said Hippy. "I know him well. He used to work for my father. He isn't half so foolish as he looks, either. As for that wagon you used as a life preserver, I am proud to say that it was once mine."

"It must have been made especially strong," observed Reddy.

"It was. Hickory and iron were the materials used, I believe. I played with it when but a toddling che-ild," continued Hippy, "and also smashed three before my father had this one made to order. 'Twas ever thus from childhood's earliest hour,'" he added mournfully. "I always had to have things made to order."

There was a shout of laughter at Hippy's last remark. From infancy Hippy had been the prize fat boy of Oakdale.

"It's only seven o'clock," said David. I move that we hunt up the girls and have a party. That is, if Grace is willing."

"That will be fine," cried Grace.

Hippy and Reddy were despatched to find Nora and Jessica. While David took upon himself the pleasant task of going for Anne. Tom remained with Grace. He had a boyish admiration for this straightforward, gray-eyed girl and made no secret of his preference for her.

Inside of an hour the sound of girls' voices outside proclaimed the fact that the boys' mission had not been in vain. The girls had been informed by their escorts of the afternoon's happenings, but Grace and Tom were obliged to tell the story all over again.

"I hope Julia Crosby's ice bath will have a subduing effect upon her," said Nora. "I am glad, of course, that she didn't lose her life, but I'm not sorry she got a good ducking. She deserved something for the way she dragged Anne into that game of crack the whip."

"Let's talk about something pleasant," proposed Reddy.

"Me, for instance," said Hippy, with a Cheshire cat grin. "I am a thing of beauty, and, consequently, a joy forever."

"Smother him with a sofa pillow!" commanded Tom. "He is too conceited to live."

Reddy seized the unfortunate Hippy by the back of the neck, while David covered the fat youth with pillows until only his feet were visible and the smothering process was carried on with great glee until Nora mercifully came to his rescue.

CHAPTER XV

A BELATED REPENTANCE

The following Monday as Grace Harlowe was about to leave the schoolroom, Julia Crosby's younger sister, one of the freshman class, handed her a note. It was from Julia, and read as follows:

"DEAR GRACE:

"Will you come and see me this afternoon when school is over? I have a severe cold, and am unable to be out of bed. I have something I must say to you that cannot wait until I get back to school.

"Your sincere friend,

"JULIA"

"Oh, dear!" thought Grace. "I don't want to go up there. Her mother will fall upon my neck and weep, and tell me I saved Julia's life. I know her of old. She's one of the weeping kind. I suppose it's my duty to go, however."

Grace's prognostication was fulfilled to the letter. Mrs. Crosby clasped her in a tumultuous embrace the moment she entered the hall. Grace finally escaped from her, and was shown up to Julia's room.

She looked about her with some curiosity. It was a light airy room, daintily furnished. Julia was lying on the pretty brass bed in one corner of the room. She wore a dressing gown of pale blue eiderdown, and Grace thought she had never seen her old enemy look better.

"How do you do, Julia?" she said, walking over to the bed and holding out her hand to the invalid.

"Not very well," responded Julia hoarsely. "I have a bad cold and am too weak to be up."

"I'm sorry," said Grace, "the wetting didn't hurt me in the least. But, of course, I wasn't in the water like you were. It didn't hurt Tom, either."

"I'm glad you are both all right," said Julia.

She looked solemnly at Grace, and then said hesitatingly, "Grace, I didn't deserve to be rescued the other day. I've been awfully mean to you." She buried her face in the bed clothing and sobbed convulsively.

"Julia, Julia, please don't cry," said Grace, her quick sympathy aroused by the distress of another. "Did you think we would leave you to drown? You would have done the same for me. Don't you know that people never think of petty differences when real trouble arises?"

She laid her hand upon the head of the weeping girl. After a little the sobs ceased and Julia sat up and wiped her eyes.

"Bring that chair over and sit down beside me, Grace. I want to tell you everything," she said. "Last year I was perfectly horrid to you and that little Pierson girl, for no earthly reason either, I thought it was smart to annoy you and torment you. After we had the quarrel that day in the gymnasium, I was really angry with you, and determined to pay you back.

"You know, of course, that I purposely tripped you the day of the basketball game. I was awfully shocked when I found you had sprained your ankle, but I was too cowardly to confess that I did it. Miss Thompson would have suspended me from school. I didn't know whether you knew that I had done it until I met you that day in the corridor, and the way you looked at me made me feel miserable. Then we got hold of your signals."

She paused.

Grace leaned forward in her chair in an agony of suspense.

"Julia," she said, "I don't care what you did to me; but won't you please say that Anne didn't give you those signals?"

"Miss Pierson did not give them to me," was the quick reply.

"I'm so glad to hear you say it," Grace answered. "I knew she was innocent, but the girls have distrusted her all year. She lost the list accidentally, you know, but they wouldn't believe that she did."

"Yes, I heard that she did," said Julia. "The list was given to me, but I am not at liberty to tell who gave it. It was not your Anne, although I was too mean to say so, even when I knew that she had been accused. I'll write you a statement to that effect if you want me to do so. That will clear her."

"Oh, Julia, will you truly? I want it more than anything else in the whole world. A statement from you will carry more weight with the girls than anything I could possibly tell them. It will convince the doubters, you know. There are sure to be some who will insist on being skeptical."

Acting under Julia's direction, Grace brought a little writing case from a nearby table, Julia opened it, selected a sheet of paper and wrote in a firm, clear hand:

"To the members of the sophomore class, and to all those whom it may concern:

"The accusation made against Anne Pierson last fall regarding the betrayal of the basketball signals to the junior team is false. Our knowledge of these signals came from an entirely different source.

"JULIA CROSBY,
Capt. Junior Team."

"And now," concluded Julia, "I have done something toward straightening out the mischief I made. Will you forgive me, Grace, and try to think of me as your friend?"

"With all my heart," replied Grace, kissing her warmly. "And I am so happy to-day. Just think, the junior and sophomore classes will be at peace at last."

The two girls looked into each other's eyes, and both began to laugh.

"After two years' war the hatchet will be buried," said Julia a little tremulously.

"Oh, Julia!" exclaimed Grace, hopping about, "I've a perfectly splendid idea!"

"What is it?" asked Julia breathlessly.

"Let's have a grand blow out and bury the hatchet with pomp and ceremony. We'll have speeches from both classes, and a perfectly gorgeous feed afterwards. You break the news to your class and I'll endeavor to get my naughty children under control once more. I believe some of them love me a little yet," she smiled.

"Of course, they do," said Julia stoutly. "I must say I don't see why they were so hateful to you, even if Anne Pierson were under suspicion. I know I am to blame for helping the grudge along," she added remorsefully, "but I am, not the only one."

"I know," said Grace quickly. "There are lots of things I'd like to say, but for certain reasons of my own I shall not say them. You understand, I think."

Julia nodded. She did, indeed, understand, and the full beauty of Grace Harlowe's nobility of spirit was revealed to her.

"You are the finest, squarest girl I ever knew, Grace," she said admiringly.

"Nonsense," laughed Grace, flushing a little at the tribute paid her by the once arrogant junior captain. "You don't know me at all. I have just as many faults as other girls, with a few extra ones thrown in. I have no claim to a pedestal. I hope we shall be friends for the rest of our schooldays and forever after. You will be a senior next year, and I shall be a junior. It's time we put by childish quarrels, and assumed the high and mighty attitude of the upper classes. It is our duty to become a living example to erring freshmen."

Both girls laughed merrily; then Grace rose to go. She kissed Julia good-bye and walked out of the house as though on air. Her cup of happiness was full to the brim. She carefully tucked the precious paper away in her bag and sped down the street on winged feet.

The incredible had come to pass. Her old-time enemy had become her friend. She wondered if it could have ever come about by any other means. She doubted it. She had always heard that "Desperate cases require desperate remedies." The happenings of the past week seemed conclusive proof of the truth of the saying. Furthermore, she believed in the sincerity of Julia Crosby's repentance. It was more than skin deep. She felt that henceforward Julia would be different. Best of all, she had the reward of her own conscience. In being true to Anne she had been true to herself.

CHAPTER XVI

AN OUNCE OF LOYALTY

When the girls of the sophomore class entered their locker-room the next day they found a notice posted to the effect that a class meeting would be held after school in the locker-room at which all members were earnestly requested to be present.

There was considerable speculation as to the object of the meeting, and no one knew who had posted the notice. Grace kept her own counsel. She wished to take the class by surprise, and thus make Anne's restoration to favor complete.

At recess Nora and Jessica brought up the subject, but found that Grace apparently wished to avoid talking about it.

"You'll attend, won't you, Grace?" asked Anne.

"Of course," said Grace hastily. "Will you excuse me, girls? I have a theorem to study."

She felt that if she stayed a minute longer she would tell her friends the good news and spoil her surprise.

"What makes Grace act so queerly to-day?" said Jessica. "I believe she knows something and won't tell us."

"I'll make her tell it," said Nora, and ran after Grace. But just then the gong sounded and recess was over.

As soon as school was dismissed for the day, the entire sophomore class crowded into the locker-room. They were curious to know what was in the wind. Every member was present, and Grace felt a secret satisfaction when Miriam Nesbit, looking rather bored, sauntered in.

There was a confused murmur of voices. The girls chattered gayly to each other, as they waited for some one to call the meeting to order. When Grace left the corner where she had been standing with her three friends, and stood facing her classmates, the talking instantly ceased.

"Girls," she said, "I suppose you wonder who called this meeting, and why it was called? I wrote the notice you all read this morning. I have something to tell you which I hope you will be glad to hear."

"At the beginning of the school year, some things happened that caused unpleasant suspicions to rest upon a member of our class. You all know who I mean. It has caused her and her friends a great deal of unhappiness, and I am glad to be able at last to bring you the proof that she has been misjudged."

Grace paused and looked about her. She noted that Miriam had turned very pale.

"Just as I suspected," thought Grace, "she really did have a hand in that signal affair."

Then she continued.

"A few days ago I had occasion to call upon the junior captain, Miss Crosby. While there, she assured me that the juniors did receive our signals, but that Miss Pierson had absolutely nothing to do with the matter. I was not sure that you would care to take my word, alone, for this" - Grace couldn't resist this one tiny thrust - "so she very kindly gave me the assurance in writing, signed by herself."

Jessie Graham Flower

Grace then unfolded the paper and in a clear voice read Julia's statement.

There was not a sound in the room. Grace stood waiting. She had done her part, the rest lay with her classmates.

Nora and Jessica had their arms around Anne, who had begun to cry quietly. The relief was so great that it had unnerved her. Then Marian Barber sprang to Grace's side and seized her by the hand.

"Listen, girls," she cried, "I want to acknowledge for the second time that I am heartily ashamed of myself. We have all been nasty and suspicious toward Anne. We never gave her a chance to defend herself, we just went ahead and behaved like a lot of silly children. I am sorry for anything I have ever said about her, and I want to tell you right here that I consider Grace Harlowe the ideal type of High School girl. I only wish I were half as noble and courageous. I suppose you all wonder why Grace went to see Julia Crosby. Well I'll tell you. I found out about it from Julia's sister this morning."

"Oh Marian, please don't," begged Grace, rosy with confusion.

But the girls cried in chorus, "Tell us, Marian! Don't mind Grace!"

When Marian had finished many of the girls were in tears. They crowded around Anne and Grace vying with each other in trying to show their good will. Then Eva Allen proposed three cheers for Grace and Anne.

They were given with a will. The noise of the ovation bringing one of the teachers to the door with the severe injunction, "Young ladies please contain yourselves. There is too much noise here."

The girls dispersed by twos and threes, until Marian Barber and the chums were the only ones left.

"I have a motto," said Marian, "that I shall bring here to-morrow and hang in the locker-room. If I had paid more attention to it it would have been better for me."

"What is it, Marian?" asked Jessica.

"Wait and see," replied Marian. "Oh, it's a good one, and appropriate, too."

After saying good-bye to Marian the four chums walked on together.

"Are you happy, Anne, dear?" said Grace, slipping her hand into Anne's.

Anne looked up at Grace with a smile so full of love and gratitude that Grace felt well repaid for all she had endured for friendship's sake.

"Everything has turned out just like the last chapter in a book," sighed Nora with satisfaction "The sinner - that's Julia Crosby - has repented, and the truly good people - Anne and Grace - have triumphed and will live happy forever after."

The girls laughed at Nora's remark.

"Now I can go on planning for our big game without being afraid that the girls will stay away from practice and do things to annoy and make it hard for me," said Grace happily. "I know that we shall win. I feel so full of enthusiasm I don't know what to do. Oh, girls, I forgot to tell you that Julia Crosby and I have a perfectly splendid plan. But I promised not to say anything to anyone about it until she comes back to school."

"How funny it sounds to hear you talk about having plans with Julia Crosby," said Jessica laughing. "You will make Miriam Nesbit jealous if you take Julia away from her."

"By the way, girls!" exclaimed Nora, "what became of Miriam? I saw her enter the locker-room, but she wasn't there when Marian Barber began her speech. I know she did not remain, because I looked for her and couldn't find her."

"I saw her go," said Grace quietly, "That is the only part of this story that doesn't end well. She doesn't like Anne or me any better than before and never will, I'm afraid. She influenced the girls against us, after the first game, and you remember what she said at the basketball meeting, don't you, Nora?"

"Yes," responded Nora, "I do, and if she hadn't been David's sister I would have told her a few plain truths, then and there."

"I said at the beginning of the year that I believed Miriam had a better self," said Grace thoughtfully. "I still believe it, and I am not going to give her up yet."

"I don't envy you the task of finding it," said Jessica.

"I wonder what Marian Barber's motto is?" mused Anne. "She said it would be a good one."

"I have no doubt of that. Marian Barber doesn't usually do things by halves when once she starts," said Jessica. "I am surprised that she ever allowed herself to be drawn into Miriam's net. She seems awfully sorry for it now."

"Oh, girls," cried Nora suddenly. "I have a half a dollar."

"Really?" said Jessica. "I didn't suppose there was that much money in Oakdale."

"My sister gave it to me this morning," Nora went on, ignoring Jessica's remark. "I am supposed to buy a new collar with it, but if you are thirsty -"

"I am simply perishing with thirst," murmured Grace.

Five minutes later the four girls were seated in the nearest drug store busily engaged with hot chocolate, while they congratulated Nora on having spent her money in a good cause.

The sophomores smiled to themselves next morning at Marian's motto. It hung in a prominent place in the locker-room and read: "An ounce of loyalty is worth a pound of cleverness."

CHAPTER XVII

BURYING THE HATCHET

It was some days before Julia Crosby was able to return to school, but when she did put in an appearance, she lost no time in taking her class in hand and bringing about a much-needed reform. The part played by Grace Harlowe in Julia's rescue had been related by her to various classmates who had visited her during her illness, and Grace found that the older girls were inclined to lionize her more than she cared to be. She received praise enough to have completely turned her head had she not been too sensible to allow it to do so.

After holding a conference with Julia, the two girls sent out notices to their respective classes that a grand reunion of the two classes would take place on the next Saturday afternoon at one o'clock, at the old Omnibus House, providing the weather permitted. A tax of twenty-five cents apiece was levied on the members of both classes. "Please pay your money promptly to the treasurer of your class," ended the notices, "if you wish to have plenty to eat. Important rites and ceremonies will be observed. You will be sorry if you stay away, as an interesting program is promised. Please keep this notice a secret."

"The field back of the Omnibus House is an ideal place for the burial," Julia told Grace. "It was there that the 'Black Monks of Asia' held their revel and were unmasked by the freshmen. Besides, it's quiet and we shan't be disturbed."

Grace agreed with her, and the two girls outlined the proceedings with many a chuckle.

The junior and sophomore classes had been requested to go directly to the Omnibus House.

"It would be great to have both classes march out there, but we should have the whole of Oakdale marching with us before we arrived at the sacred spot," observed Grace, with a giggle.

"If we don't have a lot of freshmen to suppress it will be surprising. I do hope the girls haven't told anyone," Julia answered. "By the way, we have a hatchet at home that will be just the thing to bury. It is more like a battle-ax than anything else, and looks formidable enough to represent the feeling that the juniors and sophomores are about to bury. Now, Grace, you must prepare a speech, for we ought to have representative remarks from both classes. Then Anne Pierson must recite 'The Bridge of Sighs,' after I have made it over to suit the occasion. We'll have to have some pallbearers. Three girls from each class will do."

Julia planned rapidly and well. Grace listened attentively. The junior captain had remarkable energy. It was easy to see why Julia had always headed her class. Julia in turn, was equally impressed with Grace's ability. A mutual admiration society bade fair to spring up between the two, so recently at swords' points.

On Saturday the weather left nothing to be desired. It seemed like a day in late spring, although it was in reality early March. At one o'clock precisely the two classes, with the exception of one member, assembled. Julia Crosby acting as master of ceremonies, formed the classes in two lines, and marched them to the middle of the field. Here, to their complete mystification, they saw a large hole about four feet in depth had been dug.

"Who on earth dug that hole, and what is it for?" inquired a curious sophomore.

"Hush!" said Julia Crosby reverently. "That is a grave. Be patient. Curb your rising curiosity. Soon you shall know all."

"Assistant Master Harlowe, will you arrange the esteemed spectators, so that the ceremony may proceed?"

Grace stepped forward and solemnly requested the girls to form a double line on each side of the opening. The shorter girls were placed in the front rows.

"The sophomores will now sing their class song," directed the master of ceremonies.

When the sophomores had finished, the juniors applauded vigorously. The juniors' song was next in order and the sophomores graciously returned the applause.

"I will now request the worthy junior members Olive Craig, Anne Green and Elsie Todd, to advance. Honorable Assistant Master Harlowe, will you name your trusted followers?"

Grace named Nora, Jessica and Marian Barber who came to her side with alacrity.

"During the brief space of time that we are obliged to absent ourselves, will every guest keep her roving eyes bent reverently on the ground and think about nothing. It is well to fittingly prepare for what is to come."

With this Julia marched her adherents down the field and around the corner of the Omnibus House. She was followed by Grace and her band. There was a chorus of giggles from the chosen helpers that was sternly checked by Julia.

Before their eyes stood a large, open paste-board box lined with the colors of both classes, in which reposed the Crosby hatchet, likened to a battle-ax by Julia. Its handle was decorated with sophomore and junior ribbons, and around the head was a wreath of immortelles. A disreputable looking sheaf of wheat lay across the end of the box.

There was a smothered laugh from Nora, whose quick brain had grasped the full significance of the thing.

"This is not an occasion for levity," reprimanded Grace sternly. "Laughing will not be tolerated."

Three twisted ribbon handles of sophomore colors and three of junior ornamented either side of the box. Each girl grasped a handle.

"We will proceed with the ceremony," directed Julia. "Lift up the box."

This was easier said than done. The handles were so close together that the girls hardly had room to step. The journey was finally accomplished without any further mishap than the sliding off of the wheat sheaf. This was hastily replaced by Jessica before its fall had been marked by the eagle eye of the master of ceremonies, who marched ahead with her assistant.

When the box had been carefully deposited at one side of the "grave," Julia Crosby took her place beside it, and assuming a Daniel Webster attitude began her address.

"Honored juniors and sophomores. We have met together to-day for a great and noble purpose. We are about to take a step which will forever after be recorded among the doughty deeds of Oakdale High School. It will go down in High School history as the glorious inspiration of a master mind. We are going to unfurl the banner of peace and bury the hatchet.

"Since the early days of our class history, war, cruel war, has raged between the august bodies represented here to-day. On this very field many moons ago the gallant sophomores advanced upon the, then, very fresh freshmen, but retreated in wild confusion. It is therefore fitting that this should be the place chosen for the burial of all grudges, jealousies and unworthy emotions that formerly rent our breasts."

Here Julia paused to take breath.

The girls cheered wildly.

Julia bowed right and left, her hand over her heart. When the noise had subsided, she continued. She bewailed junior misdeeds and professed meek repentance. She dwelt upon the beauty of peace and she begged her hearers henceforth to live with each other amicably.

It was a capital address, delivered in a mock-serious manner that provoked mirth, and did more toward establishing general good feeling than any other method she might have tried. In closing she said:

"The hatchet is the symbol of war. The wheat-sheaf represents our elderly grudge; but the immortelles are the everlasting flowers of good will that spring from the planting of these two. We will now listen to a few remarks from the pride of the sophomore class, Assistant Master of Ceremonies Grace Harlowe."

Grace attempted to speak, but received an ovation that made her flush and laughingly put her hands over her ears. When she was finally allowed to proceed, she delivered an oration as flowery as that of the master of ceremonies.

When the cries of approbation evoked by Grace's oration had died away, it was announced that the "renowned elocutionist," Miss Anne Pierson, would recite a poem appropriate to the occasion. Anne accordingly recited "The Bridge of Sighs," done over by Julia Crosby, and beginning:

"Take it up gingerly;
Handle with care;

'Tis a relic of sophomore
And junior warfare."

The intense feeling with which Anne rendered this touching effusion, caused the master of ceremonies to sob audibly and lean so heavily upon her assistant for support that that dignified person almost pitched head first into the opening, and was saved from an ignominious tumble by one of her attendants. This was too much for the others, who, forgetting the solemnity of their office, shrieked with mirth, in which the spectators were not slow to join.

"I think we had better wind up the ceremony," said Julia with great dignity. "These people will soon be beyond our control."

The attendants managed to straighten their faces long enough to assist in the concluding rites that were somewhat hastily performed, and the master of ceremonies and her assistants held an impromptu reception on the spot.

"Now," said Julia Crosby, "we have done a good day's work for both classes. I only hope that no prying freshmen hear of this. They will be sure to come here and dig up what we have gone to such pains to bury. They have no respect for their superiors. However, you have all behaved yourselves with true High School spirit, and I wish to announce that you will find a spread awaiting you around the corner of the Omnibus House."

There was a general hurrah at this statement, and the guests rushed off to the spot designated.

Grace had held an earnest conference with old Jean, and the result showed itself in the row of tables rudely constructed to fit the emergency. He it was who had dug the "grave." He now sat on the steps waiting to build a fire, over which Grace had planned to make coffee for the hungry girls whose appetites had been whetted by the fresh air.

The money contributed by the classes had been used to good advantage by Grace and Julia, and piles of tempting eatables gladdened the eyes of the guests.

For the next half hour feasting was in order. Juniors and sophomores shared cups; as the supply of these were limited. At the end of that time the last crumb of food had disappeared and the girls stood in groups or walked about the field, discussing the various features of school life.

Some one proposed playing old-fashioned games, and soon "puss in the corner," "pom-pom-pull-away," and "prisoner's goal" were in full swing.

"This brings back one's Grammar School days, doesn't it?" said Nora to Grace. They were deep in a game of prisoner's goal, and stood for a moment waiting for the enemy to move toward them.

"I haven't had such a good, wholesale romp for ages," answered Grace, and was off like the wind to intercept Eva Allen as she endeavored to make a wide detour of their goal.

The hours slipped by on wings.

The start home was made about five o'clock. The juniors and sophomores trooped back to Oakdale arm in arm, singing school songs and making the welkin ring with their joyous laughter.

The people of Oakdale smiled at the procession of happy girls and wondered what particular celebration was in order.

When the center of town was reached the party broke up with a great deal of laughing and chattering, the girls going their separate ways in the best of spirits.

"I've had a perfectly fine time," declared Grace, as she said good-bye to her chums, "and how glad I am that we are all friends again."

She quite forgot when she made that statement that Miriam Nesbit had not honored the reunion with her presence.

Jessie Graham Flower

CHAPTER XVIII

AT THE ELEVENTH HOUR

One more excitement was to quicken the pulses of the sophomores before they settled down to that long last period of study between Easter holidays and vacation.

The great, decisive basketball game with the juniors was now to take place.

Grace, in conclave with her team, had gone over her instructions for the hundredth time. They had discussed the strong points of the juniors and what were their own weak ones.

Miriam Nesbit was sullen at these meetings; but in the practice game she had played with her usual agility and skill, so the girls felt that she was far too valuable a member of the team for them to mind her humors.

"Everybody is coming to-morrow to see us play," exclaimed Nora in the locker-room, at the recess on Friday. "I don't believe the President's visit would create more excitement, really," she added with a touch of pride.

"Did you know," interposed Anne, "that the upperclass girls are calling Grace and Julia Crosby 'David and Jonathan'?"

This was also an amusing piece of news at which the other girls laughed joyously. In fact, there was no such feeling of depression before this game as had affected the class when the first game was played. The sophomores were cheerful and confident, awaiting the great battle with courage in their hearts.

"Be here early, girls," cautioned Grace, as they parted after school that day. "Perhaps we may get in a little practice before the people begin to come."

Grace hurried through her own dinner as fast as she could, on the eventful Saturday.

"I shall be glad when this final game is over, child," exclaimed Mrs. Harlowe anxiously, "I really think you have had more athletics this winter than has been good for you, what with your walking, and skating, dancing, and now basketball."

"You'll come, won't you, mother?" cried Grace, seizing her hat and rushing off without listening to Mrs. Harlowe's comments. "We are sure to win," she called as she waved her a good-bye kiss.

There was no one in the school building when Grace got back; that is, no one except the old janitress, who was sweeping down the corridor, as usual. The other girls had not been so expeditious and Grace found the locker-room deserted.

With trembling eagerness she was slipping on her gymnasium suit and rubber-soled shoes, when she suddenly remembered that she had left her tie in the geometry classroom. She had bought a new one the day before, placed it in the back of her geometry and walked out of the classroom, leaving book, tie and all behind.

"I'll run up and get it right away, before the others come," she said to herself.

Running nimbly up the broad stairway, she entered the

deserted classroom and hurried down the aisle to the end of the room where she usually sat during recitation.

"Here it is," she murmured, taking it out of the book and tying it on. Then, sitting down at the desk, she rested her chin in her hands. The quiet of the place was soothing to her excited nerves, and since it was so early she would rest there for a moment and think.

Grace might have dreamed away five minutes when she heard the distant sound of voices below.

"Dear me," she exclaimed, laughing, "they'll scold me for not being on time. I must hurry." So she hastened up the aisle to the door, which was shut, although she had not remembered closing it after her.

She turned the knob, still smiling to herself, but the door stuck fast. It was locked!

Grace was so stunned that for a moment she hardly comprehended what had happened. She sat down and tried to collect her thoughts. Locked up in an upper classroom on the afternoon of the great game!

She tried the one other door in the room. It also was locked. As for the great windows, they were too large for her to push up without a pole.

"I'll try calling," she said. "They may hear me."

But her calls were fruitless, and beating and knocking on the door panels seemed nothing but muffled sounds in the stillness.

"Oh! Oh!" she cried, rushing wildly from doors to windows and back again. "What shall I do! What shall I do?"

In the meantime, it was growing late. The sophomores had

assembled and were confidently waiting for their captain.

"She's late for the first time," observed one of the girls, "but we'll forgive her under the circumstances."

"Maybe she's in the gymnasium," suggested Anne, hurrying off to look for her friend. In spite of herself she felt some misgivings and she meant to lose no time in finding her beloved Grace.

The gallery was already half full of people. Anne moved about looking for David, or some one who could help her. Just then Mrs. Harlowe appeared at the door.

"Where is Grace, Mrs. Harlowe?" Anne demanded eagerly.

"I don't know, dear," answered Mrs. Harlowe "She ate her dinner and went off in such a hurry that I hardly had time to speak to her. She told me she wanted to get back to meet the girls."

Anne ran back to the locker-room.

"Grace left home hours ago," she cried. "I just felt that something had happened."

Jessica opened Grace's locker.

"Grace must be in the building," she exclaimed "Here are her clothes."

The girls began to rush about wildly, looking for their captain in the various rooms on the basement floor.

In a few moments a junior came to the door.

"The game will be called in ten minutes," she said. "Are you ready?"

"Yes," answered Nora calmly. "Be careful," she whispered. "Don't let them know yet."

Anne ran again to the gymnasium.

"I'll get David this time," she said to herself. "Something will have to be done if Grace is to be found in time."

David was sitting at one side of the gallery with Reddy and Hippy.

He looked very grave when Anne whispered the news to him. The place was packed with impatient spectators. The junior team was already standing on the floor talking in low voices as they waited impatiently for their opponents to appear at the opposite end.

"She must be somewhere in the building," David ejaculated. "That is if she has on her gymnasium suit. Have you looked upstairs yet?"

"No," replied Anne, "but we have been all through the down-stairs' rooms."

As they ran up the steps they heard the shrill whistle that summoned the players to their positions.

"Come on," cried Nora. "Miriam, you will have to take Grace's place, and Eva Allen will substitute for you."

It still lacked a few moments of the toss up; the whistle having been blown sooner to hurry the dilatory sophomores, who seemed determined to linger, unaccountably, in the little side room.

But in that brief time a remarkable change had taken place in the demeanor of Miriam Nesbit. Two brilliant spots burned on her cheeks, and her black eyes flashed and glowed with happiness. The other girls were too downcast and wretched to notice the transformation. They walked slowly into the gymnasium and stood, ill at ease and downcast, at their end of the hall.

A wave of gossip had spread quickly over the audience, that sat waiting with breathless interest for the appearance of the tardy sophomore.

What had happened? Had there been an accident?

No; it was all a mistake. There they were. And tremendous applause burst forth, which died down almost as soon as it had begun. Where was Grace Harlowe, the daring captain of the sophomore team, who had boasted that her team would win the game if it took their last breath to do it?

There was a great craning of necks as the spectators looked in vain for the missing Grace.

Hippy dropped his chin upon his breast disconsolately.

"I feel limp as a rag," he groaned. "Where, oh, where, is our gallant captain? I'll never believe Grace deserted her post."

In the meantime poor Grace, locked in the upper classroom, had concentrated all her thoughts and mental energies on a means of making her escape in time. She sat down quietly, and, folding her hands, began to consider the situation. In looking back long afterwards upon this tragic hour, it seemed to her that it was the blackest moment of her life. The walls were thick. The doors heavy and massive. The ceilings high. There was no possibility of her cries being heard below. It is true she might break a window, but what good would that do? She couldn't jump down three stories into a stone court below. She went to the window and looked out.

"If I hung by this window sill," Grace said aloud, "I believe my feet would just reach the cornice of the second-story window."

Jessie Graham Flower

Seizing a heavy ruler from one of the desks, she ran to the window and deliberately smashed out all the plate glass in the lower sash. Then, hoisting herself onto the sill, she looked down from what seemed to be rather a dizzy height. But nerve and determination will accomplish anything, and Grace turned her eyes upward.

"I shall do it," she kept saying to herself over and over.

Clinging to the window sill, she gradually let herself down until her feet touched the top of the cornice underneath. Then, steadying herself she looked down. The cornice ledge was quite broad; broad enough to kneel on, in fact. She was glad of this, for she had intended to kneel on it, whatever its width.

With infinite caution, she gradually slipped along the ledge until she was kneeling. Resting her elbows on the stone shelf, she lowered herself to the next window sill. There she stood for a moment, looking in at the empty classroom.

The door into the corridor stood open, and as she clung to the narrow ledge, her face pressed against the window, she wondered how she was going to get in.

"Unless I butt my head against this plate glass," she exclaimed, "I really don't think I can make it. I can't kick in the glass, for fear of losing my balance."

Suddenly she heard her name called.

"Grace! Grace! Where are you?"

First it was David's voice, and then Anne's, and then the two together, echoing through the empty corridors and classrooms.

"I'm here," she answered. "Help! Help!"

Fortunately, they were passing the door at that instant and

heard her muffled cries.

"Here," she cried again, and they saw her at last, clinging desperately to the window ledge.

"I don't dare open the window," exclaimed David, thinking aloud. "The slightest jar might make her lose her balance. Grace," he cried, "I'll have to break out the upper sash. Lower your head as much as possible and close your eyes."

Another instant, and Grace was crouching in a shower of broken glass, which fell harmlessly on her back and the top of her head. David knocked off the jagged pieces at the lower end, and Grace climbed ni mbly over the sash.

"There's no time for explanations now," she cried. "I was mysteriously locked in. Has the game been called?"

David looked hurriedly at his watch.

"You have just a minute and a half," he exclaimed, and the three ran madly down the steps and into the gymnasium just as the whistle blew and the girls took their places.

When Grace, covered with dust, a long, red scratch across one cheek, rushed into the gymnasium, wild applause shook the walls of the building, for the honor of the sophomore class was saved.

CHAPTER XIX

THE GREAT GAME

It was a pitched battle from the very beginning.

The junior team was in splendid trim, and they played with great finish and judgment; but the sight of Grace, one side of whose face was tinged with blood that had risen to the surface from the deep scratch, seemed to spur the sophomores to the most spectacular and brilliant plays.

Only one girl lagged, and was not in her usual trim. It was Miriam Nesbit, whose actions were dispirited and showed no enthusiasm. Her shooting was so inaccurate that a wave of criticism spread over the audience, and the members of her own class watched her with deep anxiety. When the first half ended, however the sophomores were two points to the good.

"Grand little players!" cried Hippy, expressing his joy by kicking both feet against the wooden walls as hard as he could, while he clapped his hands and roared with all his might.

"The gamest little team I ever saw," answered Reddy.

But David, who had resumed his seat beside them, made no reply. He rose presently and went to find his sister, who was sitting somewhat apart from the other girls in gloomy silence.

"What's the matter with you, sister?" he asked gently. "You are not playing as well as usual. I expected you, especially, to do some fine work to-day. On the contrary, you have never played worse."

Miriam looked at her brother coldly.

"Why should I help them when they have dishonored me?" she demanded fiercely.

"How have they dishonored you, Miriam?" asked David.

"By making me the last in everything; putting me at the foot," she said, stifling a sob of anger.

David looked at his sister sorrowfully. He saw there was no reasoning with her in her present state of mind; yet knowing her revengeful spirit, he dreaded the consequences.

"Miriam," he said at last, speaking slowly, "perhaps, some day, you will learn by experience that the people who give a square deal are the only ones who really stay at the head. They always win out; and those who are not on the level -" He stopped. A sudden suspicion had come into his mind.

"You don't mean to say that it was you who -"

But he didn't finish. Instead, he turned on his heel and walked away. In one glance he had read Miriam's secret. Now he understood that look of wild appeal, baffled rage, mortification and disappointment, all jumbled together in her turbulent soul.

"Did she really want it so badly as all that?" he thought, "or was it only her insatiable desire never to be beaten?"

In the meantime, Grace, surrounded by a circle of her school-fellows, was telling them the history of her imprisonment. Miss Thompson and Mrs. Harlowe had made their way across the floor to the crowd of sophomores; Mrs. Harlowe to find out whether her daughter's cheek had been seriously cut, which it had not, and the principal to ask a few questions.

"Did it look like a trick, Grace?" she asked when she had heard the story.

"I hardly know, Miss Thompson. I feel certain that I left the door open when I went in. The janitress may have locked it without seeing me."

"Perhaps," answered Miss Thompson thoughtfully, "but the rule of locking the larger classrooms after school hours has never been followed that I know of. There is really no reason for it, and it might cause some delay in the morning, in case Mrs. Gunby were not around to unlock the doors."

"You will have to send a bill to father for all the broken glass," laughed Grace. "I shouldn't have been here at this moment if I hadn't done some smashing."

Miss Thompson smiled.

"You were perfectly right to do it, my dear. It was an exhibition of good judgment and great courage. As for the bill, certainly the victim of an employe's stupidity should not be held accountable for costs. But we won't disturb you now with any more questions. You deserve to win the game and I hope with all my heart you will."

There was still a little time left and Grace determined to improve those shining moments by having a talk with Miriam.

Miriam never looked up when Grace approached her. Her dark brows were knit in an ugly frown and her eyes were on the floor.

"Miriam, aren't you glad I got out of prison in time?" asked Grace cordially.

"I suppose so," answered Miriam, looking anywhere but at Grace.

"Is there anything the matter with you to-day?" continued Grace.

"No," answered Miriam shortly.

"Your playing is not up to mark. The girls are very uneasy. Won't you try to do a little better next half?"

There was a childlike appeal in Grace's voice that grated so on Miriam's nerves, at that moment that she deliberately turned and walked away, leaving Grace standing alone.

"Wait a minute, Miriam," called Nora, who, with some of the other sophomores, had been watching the scene. "You aren't ill to-day, are you?"

"No," replied Miriam angrily.

"Because, if you are really ill, you know," continued Nora, "your sub. could take your place. Anna Ray can play a great deal better game than you played the first half."

Miriam turned on Nora furiously, and was about to make one of her most violent replies, when the whistle blew and the girls flew to their places.

Julia Crosby and Grace smiled at each other in the most friendly fashion as they stood face to face for the last time that season. There was nothing but good-natured rivalry between them now.

The referee balanced the ball for an instant, her whistle to her lips. Then the ball shot up, her whistle sounded and the great decisive last half had begun.

Grace managed to bat the ball as it descended in the direction of one of her eager forwards who tried for the basket and just missed it. The juniors made a desperate attempt to get the ball into their territory, but the sophomores were too quick for them, and Nora made a brilliant throw to goal that caused the sophomore fans to cheer with wild enthusiasm.

It was a game long to be remembered. Both teams fought with a determination and spirit that caused their fans in the gallery to shout themselves hoarse. The juniors made some plays little short of marvellous, and five minutes before the last half was over the score stood 8 to 6 in favor of the sophomores.

"This game will end in a tie if they're not careful," exclaimed Hippy. "No, Nora has the ball! She'll score if anyone can! Put her home, Nora!" he yelled excitedly.

Nora was about to make one of the lightning goal throws for which she was noted, when like a flash Miriam Nesbit seized the ball from her, and attempted to make the play herself. But her aim was inaccurate. The ball flew wide of the basket and was seized by a junior guard. The tie seemed inevitable.

A groan went up from the gallery. Then a distinct hiss was heard, and a second later the entire sophomore class hissed Miriam Nesbit.

Miss Thompson rose, thinking to call the house to order, but sat down again, shaking her head.

"They know what they are about," she said, for Grace herself did not know the game any better than the principal. "It was inexcusable of Miriam, inexcusable and intentional. In attempting to gratify her own vanity she has prevented her side from scoring at a time when all personal desire should be put aside. She really deserves it."

But the score was not tied after all, for the junior guard fumbled the ball, dropped it and before she could regain possession of it, it was speeding toward Marian Barber, thrown with unerring accuracy by Grace. Up went Marian's hands. She grasped it, then hurled it with all her might, straight into the basket. Five seconds later the whistle blew, with the score 10 to 6.

The sophomores had won.

The enthusiastic fans of both classes rushed out of the gallery and down the stairs to the gymnasium. Two tall sophomores seized Grace and making a chair of their hands, carried her around the gymnasium, followed by the rest of the class, sounding their class yell at the tops of their voices.

The story of Grace's imprisonment and escape out of the third story window went from mouth to mouth, and her friends eagerly crowded the floor in an effort to speak to her. There were High School yells and class yells until Miss Thompson was obliged to cover her ears to deaden the noise.

Miss Thompson made her way through the crowd to where Grace was standing in the midst of her admiring schoolmates. The principal took the young captain in her arms, embracing her tenderly.

Surely no one had ever seen Miss Thompson display so much unrestrained and candid emotion before. There were tears in her eyes, her voice trembled when she spoke.

"It was a great victory, Grace, I congratulate you and your class. You have fought a fine, courageous battle against great odds. Many another girl who had climbed out of a third-story window, without even a rope to hold by, would have little strength left to play basketball much less to win the championship. I am very proud of you to-day, my dear," and she kissed Grace right on the deep, red scratch that marred her cheek.

"She is a girl after my own heart," Miss Thompson was thinking, as she hurried to her office. "Grace has faults, of course, but on the other hand, she is as honest as the day, modest about her ability, unselfish and with boundless courage. Certainly she is a splendid influence in a school, and I wish I had more pupils like her."

It was with difficulty that Grace extricated herself from her admiring friends and, accompanied by her chums, made for the locker room to don street attire.

Now that it was all over the reaction had set in, and she began to feel a little tired, although she was almost too happy for words. She walked along, dimly alive to what the girls were saying.

Nora was still upset over Miriam Nesbit's lawless attempt to score, and sputtered angrily all the way down the corridor. "I should think Miriam Nesbit would be ashamed to show her face in school, again, after this afternoon's performance," Nora declared.

"Did you see what David did?" queried Jessica.

"Yes, I did," said Anne.

"What was it?" asked Grace, coming out of her day dream.

"The minute the girls began to hiss Miriam, he got up and walked out of the gymnasium," Jessica replied. "I believe he was so deeply ashamed of what she did that he couldn't bear to stay."

"Well, he found Grace, and rescued her in time for the game," said Anne. "That must be some consolation to him. I don't see how you got locked in, Grace. Are you sure you didn't close the door after you. It has a spring lock, you know."

"I thought I left it open," mused Grace, "but I might have unconsciously pulled it to."

"It is very strange," replied Anne, in whose mind a vague

suspicion had taken root. Then she made a mental resolve to do a little private investigating on her own account.

When Grace reached home that night she found two boxes awaiting her.

"Oh, what can they be?" she cried in great excitement, for it was not every day that she found two imposing packages on the hall table, at the same time, addressed to her.

"Open them and see, little daughter," replied Grace's father, pinching her unscratched cheek.

The one was a large box of candy from her classmates, the contents of which they helped to devour the next day.

The other box held a bunch of violets and lilies of the valley. In this were two cards, "Mrs. Robert Nesbit" and "Mr. David Nesbit."

"Poor old David!" thought Grace, as she buried her nose in the violets. "He is trying to atone for Miriam's sins."

Jessie Graham Flower

CHAPTER XX

A PIECE OF NEWS

After the excitement of the famous game came a great calm. The various teachers privately congratulated themselves on the marked improvement in lessons, and were secretly relieved with the thought that basketball was laid on the shelf for the rest of the school year.

Miriam Nesbit left Oakdale for a visit the Monday after the game, and did not return for two weeks. The general opinion seemed to be that she was ashamed of herself; but the expression on her face when she did return was not indicative of either shame or humility. She was more aggressive than before, and looked as though she considered the whole school far beneath her. She refused to even nod to Grace, Nora, Anne or Jessica, while Julia Crosby remarked with a cheerful grin that she guessed Miriam had forgotten that they had ever been introduced.

During the Easter holidays, Tom Gray came down and his aunt gave a dinner to her "adopted children" in honor of her nephew. Nora gave a fancy dress party to about twenty of her friends, while Grace invited the seven young people to a straw ride and a moonlight picnic in Upton Wood.

The days sped swiftly by, and spring came with her wealth of bud and bloom. During the long, balmy days Grace inwardly chafed at schoolbooks and lessons. She wanted to be out of doors. As she sat trying to write a theme for her advanced English class, one sunny afternoon during the latter part of April, she glanced frequently out the window toward the golf links that lay just beyond the High School campus. How she wished it were Saturday instead of only Wednesday. That very day she had arranged to play a game of golf with one of the senior class girls, who had made a record the previous year on the links. Grace felt rather flattered at the notice of the older girl, who was considered particularly exclusive, and rarely if ever paid any attention to the lower class girls. She had accidentally learned that Grace was an enthusiastic golfer, and therefore lost no time in asking her to play.

"I was awfully surprised when she asked me to play," confided Grace to her chums on the way home from school that afternoon.

"Oh, that's nothing," said Jessica. "She ought to feel honored to think you consented. You are really an Oakdale celebrity, you know."

"Please remember when you are basking in the light of her senior countenance that you once had friends among the sophomores," said Nora in a mournful tone.

"I consider both those remarks verging on idiotic," laughed Grace. "Don't you, Anne?"

"Certainly," replied Anne. "But let me add a word of caution. Don't allow this mark of senior caprice to turn your head. Remember you are -"

"You're worse than the others," cried Grace, "Let's change the subject."

Saturday proved a beautiful day, and with a light heart Grace started for the links with her golf bag strapped across her shoulder. The senior whose name was Ethel Post, sat waiting for her on one of the rustic benches set under a tree at one side of the starting place. She greeted Grace cordially and the two girls set to work without delay to demonstrate their prowess as golfers. The caddies, two small boys of Oakdale, who could be hired at the links by anyone desiring their services, carried the girls' clubs and hunted lost balls with alacrity.

Miss Post found that Grace was a foeman worthy of her steel. The young girl's arm was steady, and she delivered her strokes with decision. Grace came out two holes ahead.

Miss Post was delighted. "I hope you will golf with me often, Miss Harlowe," she said cordially. "It is so seldom one finds a really good player."

"I am fond of all games and outdoor sports," replied Grace, "but I like basketball best of all. Did you attend any of our games during the winter, Miss Post?"

"No," answered the senior. "I am not much interested in basketball. I really paid no attention to it this year, and haven't attended a game since I was a freshman. Speaking of basketball," continued Miss Post, "I picked up a paper last fall with a whole lot of basketball plays written on it. It was labeled 'Sophomore basketball signals,' and I turned it over to one of the girls in your class. She happened to be on the team, too, and seemed very glad to get it. I presume it was hers, although she didn't say so."

At the mention of the word signals, Grace pricked up her ears. As Miss Post innocently told of finding the list, Grace could hardly control herself. She wanted to get up and dance a jig on the green. She was about to learn the truth at last.

Trying to keep the excitement she felt out of her voice, Grace asked in a low tone, "Whom did you return it to, Miss Post?"

"Why, Miss Nesbit," was the answer. "I was inside the campus when I found it, and just then she passed me on the walk. I knew she was a sophomore, and thought it best to get rid of it, as I would probably have forgotten all about it, and it never would have been returned."

"Quite true," Grace replied, but she thought to herself that a great deal of unhappiness might have been avoided if Miss Post had only forgotten.

The talk drifted into other channels. Miss Post told Grace that she expected to sail for Europe as soon as school was over. In the fall she would return and enter Wellesley. She had crossed the ocean once before, and had done the continent. This time she intended to spend all of her time in Germany. Grace decided her new acquaintance to be a remarkably bright girl. At any other time she would have listened to her with absorbed interest, but try as she might, Grace could not focus her attention on what was being said. One thought was uppermost in her mind, that Miriam was the real culprit.

What was to be done about it? She would gain nothing by exposing Miriam to her classmates. There had been too much unpleasantness already. If there was only some way that Miriam could be brought to see the folly of her present course. Grace decided to tell Anne the news that night and ask her advice.

Jessie Graham Flower

CHAPTER XXI

ANNE AND GRACE COMPARE NOTES

During the walk home from the links, Grace kept continually thinking, "I knew it was Miriam. She gave them to Julia." She replied rather absent-mindedly to Miss Post's comments, and left the older girl with the impression that Miss Harlowe was not as interesting as she had at first seemed.

Grace escaped from the supper table at the earliest opportunity, and seizing her hat, made for Anne's house as fast as her feet would take her. Anne opened the door for her.

"Oh, Anne, Anne! You never can guess what I know!" cried Grace, before she was fairly inside the house.

"Of course, I can't," replied Anne, "any more than you can guess what I know."

"Why, do you know something special, too?" demanded Grace.

"I do, indeed. But tell me your news first, and then I'll tell you mine," said Anne, pushing Grace into a chair.

"Mine's about Miriam," said Grace soberly.

"So is mine," was the reply, "and it's nothing creditable, either."

"Well," began Grace, "you know I went over to the golf links to-day with Ethel Post of the senior class."

Anne nodded.

"We were sitting on a bench resting after the game, and the subject of basketball came up. Before I knew it, she was telling me all about finding the list of signals you lost last fall. She gave them to one of our class, you can guess who."

"Miriam," said Anne.

"Yes, it was Miriam. I always suspected that she had more to do with it than anyone else. She gave Julia the signals, because she wanted to see me humiliated, and fastened suspicion on you to shield herself. She knew that I had boasted, openly, that my team would win. When Julia gave me the statement that cleared you in the eyes of the girls, she told me that she was under promise not to tell how she obtained the signals. But I'm sure she knew that I suspected Miriam. What do you think we ought to do about it?"

Grace looked anxiously at Anne.

"I don't know, yet," Anne replied. "Now listen to my news. I have felt ever since the game that your getting locked up was not accidental. I don't know why I felt so, but I did, nevertheless. So I set to work to find out if any one else had been around there that day. I went to the janitress and asked her if she had noticed any one in the corridors before halfpast one. That was about the time that people began to come, you know. She said she hadn't. She was down in the basement and didn't go near the upstairs classrooms until after two o'clock. But when she did go up there she found this."

Anne held up a curious scarab pin that Grace immediately recognized. It was one that Miriam Nesbit often wore, and was extremely fond of.

"It's Miriam's," gasped Grace. "I wonder why -" She stopped. The reason Miriam had not made her loss known was plain. She was afraid to tell where and when she had lost her pin.

"I see," said Grace slowly. "It looks pretty bad, doesn't it? But why didn't the janitress take it straight to Miss Thompson? That's what she usually does with articles she finds."

"She missed seeing Miss Thompson that Saturday," said Anne. "When I hunted her up early Monday morning, in order to question her, she asked me if I had lost a pin. She said she had just returned one to Miss Thompson, and told me where she found it. I asked her to describe the pin, and at once recognized it. Every girl in school knows that scarab of Miriam's. There is nothing like it in Oakdale.

"For a minute I didn't know what to do. Don't you remember when Miriam first had it? She showed it to Miss Thompson, and Miss Thompson spoke of how curious it was. I knew that Miss Thompson would not be apt to forget it. I hurried up to her office and found her with the pin in her hand. She had sent for Miriam, but the messenger came back with the report that Miriam wasn't in school. She laid the pin down and said, 'What is it, Anne?' So I just asked her if she would let me have the pin. Of course, she looked surprised, and asked me if I knew to whom it belonged. I told her I did. Then she looked at me very hard, and asked me to tell her exactly why I wanted it. But, of course, I couldn't tell her, so I didn't say anything. Then she said: 'Anne, I know without being told why you want this pin. I am going to give it to you, and let you settle a delicate matter in your own way. I am sure it will be the right one.'"

"Anne Pierson, you bad child!" exclaimed Grace. "To think that you've kept this to yourself ever since the game. Why didn't you tell me?"

"I wanted to think what to do about it, before telling even you," Anne replied. "Yesterday I had a long talk with David.

He knows everything that Miriam has done since the beginning of the freshman year. He feels dreadfully about it all. I think you and I ought to go to her and tell her that we are willing to forget the past and be her friends."

"It would do no good," said Grace dubiously. "She would simply laugh at us. I used to have dreams about making Miriam see the evil of her ways, but I have come to the conclusion that they were dreams, and nothing more."

"Let's try, anyway," said Anne. "David says she seems sad and unhappy, and is more gentle than she has been for a long time."

"All right, we'll beard the lion in her den, the Nesbit on her soil, if you say so. But I expect to be routed with great slaughter," said Grace with a shudder. "When do we go forth on our mission of reform?"

"We'll call on her to-morrow after school," Anne replied, "and don't forget that you once made the remark that you thought Miriam had a better self. You told me the day you read Julia Crosby's statement to the girls that you wouldn't give her up."

"I suppose that I shall have to confess that I did say so," laughed Grace. "But that was before she locked me up. She is so proud and stubborn that she will probably take the olive branch we hold out and trample upon it. After all, it really isn't our place to hold out olive branches anyway. She is the one who ought to eat humble pie. I feel ashamed to think I have to tell her what I know about her."

"So do I," responded Anne. "It's horrid to have to go to people and tell them about their misdeeds. I wouldn't propose going now if it weren't for David. He seems to think that she would be willing to behave if some one showed her how."

"All right," said Grace, "we'll go, but if we encounter a human tornado don't say I didn't warn you."

"That's one reason I want to go to her house," replied Anne. "If we approach her at school she is liable to turn on us and make a scene, or else walk off with her nose in the air. If we can catch her at home perhaps she will be more amenable to reason. But, if, to-morrow, she refuses to melt and be forgiven, then I wash my hands of her forever."

CHAPTER XXII

A RESCUE AND A REFORM

It was with considerable trepidation that Anne and Grace approached the Nesbit gate the following afternoon.

"I feel my knees beginning to wobble," Grace observed, as they rang the bell. "This business of being a reformer has its drawbacks. How had we better begin?"

"I don't know, the inspiration to say the right thing will probably come, when we see her," said Anne.

"If she behaves in her usual manner, I shall have a strong inspiration, to give her a good shaking," said Grace bluntly.

To their relief, the maid who answered the bell informed them that Miriam had gone out for a walk.

"Do you know which way she went?" Grace asked.

"I think, miss, that she went toward Upton Wood. She often walks there," replied the maid.

The girls thanked her and started down the walk.

"Miriam ought never to walk, alone, in Upton Wood, especially this time of year," remarked Grace. "There are any amount of tramps lurking around. If David knew it he would

162   Jessie Graham Flower

be awfully provoked."

"Let's walk over that way, and perhaps we'll meet her," suggested Anne. "Now that we've started, I hate to turn back. If we don't see her to-day, we'll keep on putting it off and end up by not seeing her at all."

"That's true," Grace agreed.

The two girls strolled along in the direction of Upton Wood, thoroughly enjoying their walk. Occasionally, they stopped to gather a few wild flowers, or listen to the joyous trill of a bird. They were at the edge of the wood, when Grace suddenly put up her hand.

"Hush!" she said. "I hear voices."

Just then the cry Help! Help! rang out.

"That's Miriam's voice," cried Grace.

Glancing quickly about for a weapon, Grace picked up a good-sized stick she found on the ground, and ran in the direction of the sound, Anne at her heels.

Miriam was struggling desperately to free herself from the grasp of a rough, unkempt fellow who had her by the arm and was trying to abstract the little gold watch that she wore fastened to her shirtwaist with a chatelaine pin.

The tramp stood with his back to the approaching girls. Before he was aware of their presence, Grace brought her stick down on his head with all the force she had in her strong, young arms.

With a howl of pain he released Miriam, whirling on his assailant. Grace hit him again, the force of her second blow knocking him over.

Before the man could regain his feet the three girls were off through the wood. They ran without looking back until fairly out in the open field.

"I don't see him," panted Grace, halting to get her breath. "I guess he's gone."

Anne was pale and trembling. The run out of the woods had been almost too much for her. As for Miriam, she was sobbing quite hysterically.

"Don't cry, Miriam," soothed Grace, putting her arm around the frightened girl. "He can't hurt you now. I am so glad that we happened along. You ought never to go into Upton Wood alone, you know."

Miriam gradually gained control of herself. Wiping her eyes, she asked, "How did you ever happen to be out here just at the time I needed help?"

"To tell the truth, we were hunting for you," Grace replied. "Your maid said that you had gone toward Upton Wood. We walked on, expecting every minute to meet you. Then we heard you scream and that's all."

"It's not all," said Miriam quickly. "I know I have been a wretch. I have made things unpleasant for you two girls ever since we started in at High School. I made fun of Anne, and tried to make her lose the freshman prize. I sent her that doll a year ago last Christmas, knowing that it would hurt her feelings. But the things I did last year aren't half as bad as all I've done this year, I gave -"

"That's just what we came to see you about, Miriam," interrupted Grace. "We know that you gave the signals to Julia, and we know that you locked me in the classroom the day of the big game."

Miriam flushed with shame and her lip quivered.

Jessie Graham Flower

Seeing her distress, Grace went on quickly:

"The janitress found your scarab pin just outside the door on the day of the game. Anne has it here for you."

Anne fumbled in her purse and drew out the pin.

"But how did you get it?" asked Miriam faintly, as she took the pin with evident reluctance.

"Miss Thompson gave it to me," Anne answered.

Miriam looked frightened. "Then she knows -"

"Nothing," said Grace softly. "As soon as Anne heard that Miss Thompson had your pin and knew where it had been found, she went right to the office and asked Miss Thompson to give it to her. Miss Thompson thought from the first that I had been the victim of a trick. Anne knew that the finding of your pin would make her suspect you. She had already sent for you when Anne reached the office. Luckily you weren't in school. Anne asked permission to return the pin to you. She wouldn't give any reason for asking. Finally Miss Thompson handed it to her, and told Anne she was sure she would do what was right."

"You owe a great deal to Anne, Miriam," Grace continued, "for if she had not gone to Miss Thompson I am afraid you would have been suspended from school. Miss Thompson would have had very little mercy upon you, for she knew about those examination papers last June."

Miriam looked so utterly miserable and ashamed at Grace's words, that Anne hastened to say:

"I would have given you your pin at once, Miriam, but you were away from school. Then David told me how unhappy you seemed. I hadn't said a word to any one about the pin until I told Grace. We decided to come and see you, and say that we were willing to 'let bygones be bygones' if you were. We thought it was right to let you know that we knew everything. There is only one other person who knows. That person is your brother."

"He knew I locked you up the day of the game," faltered Miriam, "The way he looked at me has haunted me ever since. He thinks me the most dishonorable girl in the world." She began to cry again.

Anne and Grace walked along silently beside the weeping girl. They thought it better to let her have her cry out. She really deserved to spend a brief season in the Valley of Humiliation.

They had now left the fields and were turning into one of the smaller streets of Oakdale.

"Miriam," said Grace, "try and brace up. We'll soon be on Main Street and you don't want people to see you cry, do you? Here," extracting a little book of rice powder paper from her bag, "rub this over your face and the marks of your tears won't show."

Miriam took the paper gratefully, and did as Grace bade her. Then she straightened up and gave a long sigh, "I feel like that man in Pilgrim's Progress, after he dropped his burden from his back," she said. "The mean things I did never bothered me until just lately. After I saw that my own brother had nothing but contempt for me, I began to realize what a wretch I was, and the remorse has been just awful."

It was David, after all, who had been instrumental in holding up the mirror so that his stubborn sister could see herself as others saw her. Although she had quarreled frequently with him, she had secretly respected his high standard of honor and fine principles. The fear that he despised her utterly had brought her face to face with herself at last.

"Anne has always wanted to be friends with you, Miriam,"

Grace said earnestly as they neared the Nesbit home. "You and I used to play together when we were little girls in the grammar school. It's only since we started High School that this quarreling has begun. Let's put it all aside and swear to be friends, tried and true, from now on? You can be a great power for good if you choose. We all ought to try to set up a high standard, for the sake of those who come after. Then Oakdale will have good reason to be proud of her High School girls."

They had reached the gate.

Miriam turned and stretched out a hand to each girl. There was a new light in her eyes. "My dear, dear friends," she said softly.

A shrill whistle broke in upon this little love feast and the three girls looked up. David was hurrying down the walk, his face aglow.

"I whistled to attract your attention. I was afraid you girls would go before I could reach you. Mother wants you girls to come in for dinner. She saw you from the window. Don't say you can't, for I'm going to call on the Piersons and Harlowes right now and inform them that their daughters are dining out to-night. So hurry along now, for mother's waiting for you."

A minute later he had mounted his motorcycle and was off down the street, going like the wind.

The girls entered the house and were warmly greeted by Mrs. Nesbit. She and David had viewed the little scene from the window. She had deeply deplored Miriam's attitude toward Grace and her chums. It was with delight that she and David had watched the three girls stop at the gate and clasp hands. She therefore hurried her son out to the girls to offer them her hospitality.

Anne had never before entered the Nesbit home. She thought it very beautiful and luxurious. Miriam put forth every effort to be agreeable, and the time passed so rapidly that they were surprised when dinner was announced.

After dinner, Miriam, who was really a brilliant performer for a girl of her age, played for them. Anne, who was a music-hungry little soul, listened like one entranced. David, seeing her absorption, beckoned to Grace, who stole softly out of the room without being observed.

Once out in the hall the two young people did a sort of wild dance to express their feelings.

"You are the best girl a fellow ever knew," said David in a whisper. "How did you do it?"

"I'll tell you some other time," whispered Grace, who had cautioned the girls to say nothing of the adventure for fear of frightening Miriam's mother. "Let's go back before they notice we're gone."

"Anne is too wrapped up in music to pay any attention to us. Come on up to my workshop. I want to show you something I'm working at in connection with my aeroplane. We can talk there, without being disturbed. I want to know what worked this transformation. It is really too good to be true. I've always wanted Miriam to be friends with Anne, but I had just about lost all hope."

Grace followed David up the stairs and through the hall to his workshop, which was situated at the back of the house.

"Now," said the young man, as he pushed forward a stool for his guest, "fire away."

Grace began with their call at the house, their walk in search of Miriam, and their adventure with the tramp, modestly making light of her own bravery. When she had finished, David held out his hand, his face glowing with appreciation "Grace," he said, "you've more spirit and courage than any girl I ever knew.

You ought to have been a boy. You would have done great things."

Grace felt that this was the highest compliment David could pay her. She had always cherished a secret regret that she had been born a girl.

"Thank you, David," she said, blushing, then hastily changed the subject. "Tell me about your aeroplane. Is it still at the old Omnibus House?"

"Yes," David answered. "I had it here all winter, but I moved it out there again about a month ago."

"I should like to see it again," said Grace. "I didn't have time to look at it carefully the day you invited us out there."

"I'll take you over any time you want to go," said David. "Oh, better still, here's a duplicate key to the place. You can take the girls and go over there whenever you please, without waiting for me. You are the only person that I'd trust with this key, Grace," he added gravely. "I had it made in case old Jean or I should lose those we carry. I wouldn't even let the fellows have one, for fear they might go over there, get careless and do some damage."

"It's awfully good of you, David," Grace replied as she took the key. "I'll be careful not to lose it. I'll put it on my watch chain. It's such a small key it is not likely it will be noticed."

Grace took from her neck the long, silver chain from which her watch was suspended. She opened the clasp, slid the key on the chain and tucked both watch and key snugly into her belt.

"There," she said, patting it, "that can't get lost. My chain is very strong. I prefer a chain to a pin or fob, because either one is so easy to lose."

"That's sensible," commented David. "Girls wouldn't be

eternally losing their watches if they weren't so vain about wearing those silly little chatelaine pins."

"Why, David Nesbit!" exclaimed Grace, glancing up at the mission clock on the wall. "It's almost nine o'clock! I had no idea it was so late. Let's go down at once."

They returned to the parlor to find Anne and Miriam deep in some foreign photographs that Miriam had collected during her trip to Europe the previous summer.

"How I should love to see Europe," sighed Anne. "I'm going there some day, though, if I live," she added with a sudden resolution.

"Mother and father have promised me a trip across as a graduation gift. Maybe you'll be able to go, too, by that time, Anne," said Grace hopefully.

"Perhaps I shall, but I'm afraid it's doubtful," said Anne, smiling a little.

"We've had a fine time, Miriam," said Grace, "but we really must go. Mother will worry if I stay any later."

"Please come again soon," said Miriam, kissing both girls affectionately. "I have a plan to talk over with you, but I can't say anything about it now. I must consult mother first. You'll like it, I'm sure."

"Of course we shall," responded Grace. "Good night, Miriam, and pleasant dreams."

"They are the nicest girls in Oakdale, and I shall try hard to be like them," thought Miriam, as she closed the door. "David is right. It certainly pays to be square."

CHAPTER XXIII

GRACE MEETS A DISTINGUISHED CHARACTER

June had come, bringing with it the trials and tribulations of final examinations. The days grew long and sunny. Roses nodded from every bush, but the pupils of Oakdale's two High Schools were far too busy to think about the beauty of the weather. Golf, tennis, baseball and other outdoor sports were sternly put aside, and the usual season of "cramming" set in. Young faces wore an almost tragic expression, and back lessons were reviewed with desperate zeal.

Grace Harlowe had crammed as assiduously as the rest, for a day or two. She was particularly shaky on her geometry. She went over her theorems until she came to triangles, then she threw the book down in disgust. "What's the use of cramming?" she said to herself. "If I keep on I won't even be able to remember that 'the hypotenuse of a right-angled triangle is equal to the sum of the squares of the other two sides.' I'm in a muddle over these triangles now. I'll find the girls and get them to go to the woods with me. I really ought to collect a few more botany specimens."

Grace's specimens were a source of keen delight to her girlish heart. She didn't care so much about pressing and mounting them. It was the joy she experienced in being in the woods that, to her, made botany the most fascinating of studies. She poked into secluded spots unearthing rare specimens. Her collection was already overflowing; still she could never resist adding just a few more.

She was doomed to disappointment as far as Nora and Jessica were concerned. Both girls mournfully shook their heads when invited to specimen-hunting, declaring regretfully they were obliged to study. Anne was at Mrs. Gray's attending to the old lady's correspondence. This had been her regular task since the beginning of the freshman year, and she never failed to perform it.

"Oh, dear, I wish examinations and school were over," Grace sighed impatiently. "I can't go to the woods alone, and I can't get any one to go with me. I suppose I'll have to give it up and go home. No, I won't, either. I'll go as far as the old Omnibus House. There are lots of wild plants in the orchard surrounding it, and I may get some new specimens."

With her basket on her arm, Grace turned her steps in the direction of the old house. She had not been there since the day of their reunion. She smiled to herself as she recalled the absurdities of that occasion.

After traversing the orchard several times and finding nothing startling in the way of specimens, Grace concluded that she might as well have stayed at home.

She walked slowly over to the steps and sat down, placing the basket beside her. "How lonely it seems here to-day," she thought. "I wonder where old Jean is? I haven't seen him for an age." Then she fell to musing over the school year so nearly ended. Everything that had happened passed through her mind like a panorama. It had been a stormy year, full of quarrels and bickerings, but it was about to end gloriously. Anne and Miriam had become the best of friends, while she and Julia Crosby were daily finding out each other's good qualities There was nothing left to be desired.

Grace started from her dream and looked at her watch. It was after six o'clock. She had better be getting back.

She rose and reached for her basket.

Suddenly a figure loomed up before her. Grace started in surprise, to find herself facing a tall, thin man with wild, dark eyes. He stood with folded arms, regarding her fixedly.

"Why, where -" but she got no further, for the curious new-comer interrupted her.

"Ah, Josephine," he said, "so I have found you at last."

"My name isn't Josephine at all. It's Grace Harlowe, and you have made a mistake," said Grace, endeavoring to pass him. But he barred her way, saying sadly:

"What, do you, too, pretend? Do you think I do not know you? I, your royal husband, Napoleon Bonaparte."

"Good gracious," gasped Grace. "He's crazy as can be. How ever shall I get away from him?"

The man heard the word "crazy" and exclaimed angrily: "How dare you call me crazy! You, of all people, should know I am sane. I have just returned from Isle of St. Helena to claim my empire. For years I have been an exile, but now I am free, free." He waved his arms wildly.

"Yes, of course I know you, now," said Grace, thinking to mollify him. "How strange that I didn't recognize you before."

Then she remembered reading in the paper of the preceding night of the escape of a dangerous lunatic from the state asylum, that was situated a few miles from Oakdale. This must be the man. Grace decided that he answered the description the paper had given. She realized that she would have to be careful not to anger him. It would require strategy to get clear of him.

"It's time you remembered me," returned Napoleon

Bonaparte, petulantly. "They told me that you had died years ago, but I knew better. Now that I have found you, we'd better start for France at once. Have you your court robes with you? And what have you done with your crown? You are dressed like a peasant." He was disdainfully eyeing her brown, linen gown.

In spite of her danger, Grace could scarcely repress a laugh. It all seemed so ludicrous. Then a sudden thought seized her.

"You see, I have nothing fit to travel in," she said. "Suppose you wait here for me while I go back to town and get my things? then I can appear properly at court."

"No you don't," said Napoleon promptly, a cunning expression stealing into his face. "If you go you'll never come back. I need your influence at the royal court, and I can't afford to lose you. I am about to conquer the world. I should have done it long ago, if those villains hadn't exiled me, and locked me up."

He walked back and forth, muttering to himself still keeping his eye on Grace for fear that she might escape.

"Oh, what shall I do?" thought the terrified girl. "Goodness knows what he'll think of next. He may keep me here until dark, and I shall die if I have to stay here until then, I must get away."

Grace knew that it would be sheer folly to try to run. Her captor would overtake her before she had gone six yards, not to mention the fit of rage her attempted flight would be likely to throw him into.

She anxiously scanned the neighboring fields in the hope of seeing old Jean, the hunter. He was usually not far away. But look as she might, she could discover no sign of him. There was only one thing in her favor. It would be light for some time yet. Being June, the darkness would not descend for two hours. She must escape, but how was she to do it!

She racked her brain for some means of deliverance, but received no inspiration. Again she drew out her watch. Then her eye rested for a second on the little key that hung on her watch chain. It was the key to the lean-to in which David kept his aeroplane. Like a flash the way was revealed to her. But would she be able to carry out the daring design that had sprung into her mind? She would try, at any rate. With an unconcern that she was far from feeling, Grace walked carelessly toward the door of the lean-to.

The demented man was beside her in a twinkling He clutched Grace by the arm with a force that made her catch her breath.

"What are you trying to do!" he exclaimed, glaring at her savagely. "Didn't I tell you that you couldn't go away!"

He held her at arm's length with one hand, and threateningly shook his finger at her.

"Remember, once and for all, that I am your emperor and must be obeyed. Disregard my commands and you shall pay the penalty with your life. What is the life of one like you to me, when I hold the fate of nations in my hands? Perhaps it would be better to put an end to you now. Women are ever given over to intriguing and deception. You might betray me to my enemies. Yet, I believed you loyal in the past. I -"

"Indeed I have always been loyal, my emperor," interrupted Grace eagerly. "How can you doubt me?"

Her situation was becoming more precarious with every minute. She must persuade this terrible individual that she was necessary to his plans, if she wished to get away with her life.

"I have your welfare constantly at heart," she continued. "Have you ever thought of flying to our beloved France? In the shed behind me is a strange ship that flies through the air. Its sails are like the wings of a bird, and it flies with the speed of the wind. It waits to carry us across the sea. It is called an aeroplane."

"I have heard of such things," said Napoleon. "When I was in exile, a fool who came to visit me showed me a picture of one. He told me it could fly like a bird, but he lied. I believe you are lying, too," he added, looking at her suspiciously.

"Let me prove to you that I am not," Grace answered, trying to appear calm, though ready to collapse under the terrible strain of the part she was being forced to play. "Do you see this key? It unlocks the door that leads to the flying ship. Would you not like to look at it?" she said coaxingly.

"Very well, but be quick about it I have already wasted too much time with you. I must be off before my enemies find me."

"You must release my arm, or I cannot unlock the door," Grace said.

"Oh, yes, you can," rejoined Napoleon, not relaxing his grip for an instant. "Do you think I am going to run any risk of losing you?"

As she turned the key he swung her to one side, and, opening the door, peered cautiously in. For a moment he stood like a statue staring in wonder at David's aeroplane, then with a loud cry that froze the blood in Grace's veins, he threw up his arms and rushed madly into the shed, shouting, "We shall fly, fly, fly!"

With a sob of terror Grace slammed the door and turned the key. She was not an instant too soon. Napoleon Bonaparte reached it with a bound and threw himself against it, uttering blood-curdling shrieks. The frightful sounds came to Grace's ears as she tore across the field in the direction of Oakdale. Terror lent wings to her feet. Every second was precious. She did not know how long the door would stand against the frantic assaults of the maniac.

She had reached the road, when, to her joy and relief, she beheld half a dozen men approaching. Stumbling blindly toward them, she panted out: "The crazy man - I - locked - him - in - the Omnibus House. Here - is - the key." She gave a long, shuddering sigh, and for the first time in her life sturdy Grace Harlowe fainted.

The men picked her up tenderly.

"Here, Hampton," said one of them, "take this child over to the nearest house. She is all in. By George, I wonder whether she has locked that lunatic up? Something has certainly upset her. We'd better get over there right away and see what we can find out."

The man addressed as Hampton picked Grace up as though she had been a baby and carried her to a house a little further up the road.

Meanwhile the men hurried on, arriving at the Omnibus House just as Napoleon succeeded in breaking down the door. Before he could elude them, he was seized by five pairs of stalwart arms. He fought like a tiger, making it difficult to bind him. This was finally accomplished though they were obliged to carry him, for he had to be tied up like a papoose to keep him from doing damage. He raved continually over the duplicity of Josephine, threatening dire vengeance when he should find her.

When Grace came to herself she looked about her in wonder. She was lying on a comfortable couch in a big, cheerful sitting room. A kindly faced woman was bathing her temples, while a young girl chafed her hands.

"Where am I?" said Grace feebly. "Did Napoleon get out?"

"Lie still and rest, my dear," said Mrs. Forrest, "Don't try to exert yourself."

Grace sat up and looked about her. "Oh, I know what happened. I fainted. How silly of me. I never did that in my life before. I had a terrible scare, but I'm all right now."

The man who had carried her to the house came forward.

"My name is Hampton, miss. I am a guard over at the asylum. Those other men you saw are employed there, too. We were looking for one of our people who escaped night before last. He nearly killed his keeper. He's the worst patient we have out there. Thinks he's Napoleon. Judging from your fright, I guess you must have met him. Did you really lock him in that old house?"

"Indeed I did," answered Grace, who was rapidly recovering from the effects of her fright. "He took me for the Empress Josephine." She related all that had happened, ending with the way she locked his emperorship in.

"Well, all I've got to say is that you're the pluckiest girl I ever came across," said the man admiringly, when Grace had finished.

But she shook her head.

"I never was so frightened in my life before. I shall never forget his screams."

It was after eight o'clock when Grace Harlowe arrived at her own door. The man Hampton had insisted on calling a carriage, so Grace rode home in state. As she neared the house she saw that the lawn and porch were full of people.

"What on earth is the matter!" she asked herself. As she alighted from the carriage her mother rushed forward and took her in her arms.

"My darling child," she sobbed. "What a narrow escape you have had. You must never, never wander off alone again."

"Why, mother, how did you know anything about it?"

"When you didn't come home to supper I felt worried, for you had not told me that you were invited anywhere. Then Nora came down to see you, and seemed surprised not to find you at home. She said you had gone on a specimen hunt after school. I became frightened and sent your father out at once to look for you. He met the keepers with that dreadful man," said Mrs. Harlowe, shuddering, "and they described you, telling him where you were and how they had met you. Your father went straight out to the Forrests. I suppose you just missed him."

Grace hugged her mother tenderly. "Don't worry, mother. I'm all right. What are all these people standing around for?"

"They came to see you, of course. The news is all over town. Everyone is devoured with curiosity to hear your story."

"It looks as though I had become a celebrity at last," laughed Grace.

She was obliged to tell the story of her adventure over and over again that night to her eager listeners. Her chums hung about her adoringly. Hippy, Reddy and David were fairly beside themselves.

"Oh, you lunatic snatcher," cried Hippy, throwing up his hat to express his feelings.

"You never dreamed that the little key you gave me would prove my salvation," said Grace to David, as her friends bade her good night. "It surely must have been fate."

CHAPTER XXIV

COMMENCEMENT

Examinations had ceased to be bug-bears and kill joys to the young idea of Oakdale. The last paper had been looked over, and the anxious hearts of the majority of the High School pupils had been set at rest. In most cases there was general rejoicing over the results of the final test. Marks were compared and plans for the next year's course of study discussed.

The juniors were about to come into their own. When the present seniors had been handed their diplomas, and Miss Thompson and Mr. Cole had wished them god-speed, the present juniors would start on the home stretch that ended in commencement, and a vague awakening to the real duties of life.

The senior class stood for the time being in the limelight of public attention. It was the observed of all observers. Teas were given in honor of its various members, and bevies of young girls in dainty summer apparel brightened the streets of Oakdale, during the long sunny afternoons.

It was truly an eventful week. Grace Harlowe gave a tea in honor of Ethel Post, which was a marked social success. The two girls had become thoroughly well acquainted over their golf and had received great benefit from each other's society. Miss Post's calm philosophical view of life had a quieting effect on impulsive Grace, while Grace's energy and whole-hearted way of diving into things proved a stimulus to the older girl.

It was Tuesday afternoon and class day. High School girls in gala attire were seen hurrying up the broad walk leading to the main door of the school building.

It was the day of all days, to those about to graduate. Of course, receiving one's diploma was the most important feature, but class day lay nearest the heart.

The exercises were to be held in the gymnasium.

The junior and senior classes had brought in half the woods to beautify the big room, and Oakdale gardens had been ruthlessly forced to give up their wealth of bud and bloom in honor of the occasion.

It was customary for the seniors to invite the junior class, who always sat in a body at one side of the gymnasium; while the seniors sat on the opposite side. The rest of the space was given up to the families of the seniors and their friends. Lucky, indeed, were those who could obtain an invitation to this most characteristic of class functions.

The four girl chums had been among the fortunate recipients of invitations. A very pretty picture they made as they followed the usher, one of the junior class, to their seats.

Grace wore a gown of pale blue organdie that was a marvel of sheer daintiness. Jessica, a fetching little affair of white silk muslin sprinkled with tiny pink rosebuds; while Anne and Nora were resplendent in white lingerie gowns. Anne's frock was particularly beautiful and the girls had exclaimed with delight over it when they first caught sight of her.

It was a present from Mrs. Gray, Anne told them. She had fully expected to wear her little white muslin, but the latter had grown rather shabby and she felt ashamed of it. Then a boy appeared with a big box addressed to her. Wrapped in fold after fold of tissue paper lay the exquisite new gown. Pinned to one sleeve was a note from Mrs. Gray, asking her to accept the gift in memory of the other Anne - Mrs. Gray's young daughter - who had passed away years ago. There were tears in Anne's eyes as she told them about it, the girls agreeing with her that there was no one in the world quite so utterly dear as Mrs. Gray.

"I'm glad we're early," whispered Nora. "We can watch the classes come in. See, that place is for the juniors. It is roped off with their colors and the other side belongs to the seniors."

"How fine the gym. looks," remarked Anne. "They certainly must have worked hard to fix it up so beautifully."

"Julia Crosby is largely responsible for it," answered Grace. "She has the most original ideas about decorations and things. You know the juniors always decorate for the seniors. It's a sacred duty."

"Did you know that Julia was elected president of her class?" asked Jessica.

"Oh, yes," said Grace, "she told me about it the other day. Oh, girls, here they come! Doesn't Ethel Post look sweet? There's Julia at the head of her class."

"It is certainly great to be a graduate," sighed Nora.

"Speaking of graduation," said Grace, "did you know that David has put off his graduation for another year! He wished to finish school with Hippy and Reddy. They have planned to enter the same college. So our little crowd will be together for one more year."

"How nice of him," cried the girls.

"Yes, isn't it! I'll be awfully sorry when my turn comes,"

responded Grace. "I'm sure I shall never care for college as I do for this dear old school."

"You can't tell until you've tried it," said Nora wisely.

The two classes had now seated themselves, and an expectant hush fell upon those assembled. The first number on the program was a song by the senior glee club. This was followed by the salutatory address, given by a tall dignified senior. The class poem came next, and was received with enthusiasm. The other numbers followed in rapid succession, each being applauded to the echo. The class grinds were hailed with keen relish. Each girl solemnly rose to take her medicine in the form of mild ridicule over some past harmless folly.

The class prophecy provoked ripples of merriment from the audience.

Grace chuckled with glee at the idea of exclusive Ethel Post becoming the proprietor of a moving-picture show at Coney Island. The futures prophesied for the other members of the class were equally remarkable for their impossibility.

At last nothing remained but the senior charge and the junior reply. The president of the senior class rose, and facing the juniors poured forth her final words of advice and counsel. She likened them to a baby in swaddling clothes, and cautioned them to be careful about standing on their feet too early. It was the usual patronizing speech so necessary to class day.

Julia Crosby smiled a little as the senior exhorted her hearers to never forget the dignity of their station. She was thinking of the day she crashed into that young woman, in the corridor. The senior president had manifested the dignity of her station then.

Julia straightened her face and stepped forward to make her reply. She thanked the president for her solicitude and tender counsel. She humbly acknowledged that the juniors were helpless infants, entirely innocent of the wicked world. They realized that they needed proper nourishment and exercise. There was one consolation however, they were daily growing larger and wiser, and their lungs were strong. If all went well they hoped to be healthy, well-grown seniors, capable of giving sage advice to those who would follow them.

Grace's face was full of eager appreciation as she listened to Julia's clever speech. How greatly she had changed, and what a power she would be in her class during the senior year. Grace felt that her sophomore year, though dark in the beginning, was about to end in a blaze of glory.

Julia sat down amid demonstrations of approval. Then the first notes of "Auld Lang Syne" sounded on the piano, and the entire audience, led by the senior glee club, rose to their feet to join in that sweetest of old songs whose plaintive melody causes heart strings to tighten and eyes to fill.

The four chums silently joined hands as they sang, and mentally resolved that with them "auld acquaintance" should never "be forgot."

There was a second's pause after the song was done. Then clear on the air rose the senior class yell. That broke the spell. Those who had felt lumps rising in their throats at the music, laughed. A buzz of conversation began, and soon the graduates were surrounded by their families and friends.

The gymnasium gradually cleared. The seniors hurried off to their banquet on the lawn and one more class day glided off to find its place with those of the past.

"Wasn't it perfectly lovely?" sighed Jessica, as they made their way out.

"I think commencement week has even more thrills in it than Christmas,"

Jessie Graham Flower

Nora replied. "Wait till we have our class day. You shall write the class poem, Anne, and Jessica the song."

"I speak for the class prophecy," said Grace.

"That leaves nothing for me but the grinds. But that job would be greatly to my taste," said Nora.

"What about the rest of the class?" inquired Anne, smiling at this monopoly of class honors. "Are we to carry off all the glory!"

"Without a doubt," Jessica answered. "After us there are no more."

"Be sure to come to my house for supper Thursday evening," said Grace. "We are to go to commencement together, you know. The boys are coming, too."

The chums parted with many expressions of satisfaction over the pleasant afternoon's entertainment.

Thursday evening found them impatiently awaiting the boys.

"I suppose they all stopped to fuss and prink," said Nora, as she peered through the vines that screened the porch. "Men are, truly, vainer than girls. There they come around the corner, now. I really believe Hippy is growing fatter. He looks awfully nice to-night, though," she hastily added.

Hippy had a friend in Nora.

"Did you know that Tom Gray is in town?" asked David, as he took his place beside Anne and Grace. The latter carried an immense bouquet of red roses to give to Ethel Post.

"Oh, how nice!" exclaimed Grace. "I suppose he'll be there to-night with dear Mrs. Gray."

"Yes, they are going," said David. "I don't believe Mrs. Gray has missed a commencement for the last twenty years."

"I wonder who'll get the freshman prize this year?" mused Grace. "I hope it goes to some girl who really needs it. I know one thing; there will be no claimant for the hundred dollar prize this year. Anne broke the record."

"Indeed she did," said David, looking fondly at Anne. "To be in company with Oakdale's star prize winner is a great honor."

"Oh, don't," said Anne who hated compliments.

"Very well, if you spurn the truth," replied David. "By the way, I have an invitation to deliver. Miriam wants all of you to come up to our house the minute the exercises are over to-night. Never mind if it is late. Commencement comes but once a year."

"De-lighted," chorused the chums.

"Hush," said Hippy. "Make no uproar. We are about to enter the sacred precincts of Assembly Hall. I feel that on account of my years of experience I must make myself responsible for the behavior of you children. Smother that giggle, Nora O'Malley," he commanded, looking at Nora with an expression of severity that set oddly on his fat, good-natured face.

This made the whole party laugh, and Hippy declared, disgustedly, that he considered them quite ignorant of the first principles of good behavior.

They were seated in the hall at last, and for the next two hours listened with serious attention to the essays and addresses of the graduates.

Grace had sent Ethel Post her roses as soon as she entered the hall, and had the pleasure of seeing them in her friend's hands.

Jessie Graham Flower

The diplomas were presented, and the freshman prize given out. It was won by a shy-looking little girl with big, pleading, brown eyes. Grace watched her closely as she walked up to receive it and resolved to find out more about her.

"She looks as though she needed friends," was her mental comment.

Anne, too, felt drawn toward the slender little girl. She recalled her freshman commencement and her total collapse after the race had been won.

"I hope that little girl has friends as good and true as mine," she whispered to Grace.

"Don't you think she looks lonely?" Grace asked.

"She surely does," returned Anne. "Let's find out all about her."

"Done," Grace replied.

As soon as the exercises were over the young people hurried over to where Tom Gray and his aunt stood talking with friends.

"Well, well," sighed the old lady joyously, "here are all my own children. I am so glad to see you. I understand that I am too late with my invitation for an after gathering. Miriam has forestalled me," she added, placing her arm around Miriam, whose face glowed with pleasure at the caress.

"She has invited me, too, so I am not to complain. As many as there are room can ride in my carriage. The rest will have go in Tom's."

"Tom's?" was the cry, "When did he acquire a carriage?"

"Come and see it," was Tom's reply.

They all trooped out, Hippy leading the van.

"I wish to be the first to look upon the miracle," he cried.

"It's a peach," he shouted, as the others came up, and he was right.

"O Tom, isn't it great?" Grace exclaimed.

Directly in front of Mrs. Gray's carriage stood a handsome Packard car.

"Aunt Rose gave it to me, to-day," he explained, his face glowing. "It has been waiting a week for me. Come on, everybody, and we'll get up steam and fly to Nesbit's."

Of course every one wanted to ride in the new car. David and Anne decided, however, to go with Mrs. Gray, and with a honk! honk! the automobile was off.

The Nesbit home was ablaze with light. Mrs. Nesbit stood in the wide hall waiting to receive Miriam's guests.

"The first thing to do is to find food," declared David, leading the way to the dining room.

The whole party exclaimed with admiration at the tastefully decorated table. A huge favor pie in the shape of a deep red rose ornamented the center, the ribbons reaching to each one's place. There were pretty, hand-painted place cards, too, tied with red and gold, the sophomore colors.

Mrs. Gray occupied the place of honor at the head of the table. She was fairly overflowing with happiness and good cheer, as she beamed on first one and then another of her children.

The young people did ample justice to the delicious repast served them. The favor pie created much amusement, as the favors were chosen to suit the particular personality of each

Jessie Graham Flower

guest. After every one had finished eating, a season of toasts followed.

"Here's to dear Mrs. Gray," said David, raising his glass of fruit punch, "May she live to be one hundred years old, and grow younger every day. Drink her down."

Mrs. Gray proposed a toast to Mrs. Nesbit, which was drunk with enthusiasm. Presently every one had been toasted, then Miriam rose and begged permission to speak.

It was unanimously granted.

"I suppose you all think I invited you here to-night for the express purpose of having a good time," she said. "So I did. But now that you are here, I want to talk to you about a plan that I hope you will like. It rests with you whether or not it materializes. You know that we have a cottage at Lake George, although we do not always spend our summers there. But I want to go there this year, and you can make it possible for me to do so."

"We'll carry your luggage and put you on the train, if that will help you out any," volunteered Hippy.

Miriam laughed. "That isn't enough," she said. "I want every one of you to go, too, Now don't say a word until I'm through. Mother has given her consent to a house party, and will chaperon us. Don't one of you refuse, for I shall pay no attention to you. You simply must come. We are to start next Tuesday, and stay as long as we like. So you'll have to make your preparations in a hurry. We'll meet at the station next Tuesday morning at 9.30. That's all."

Then what a babble arose. Grace and Nora were in high glee over the proposed trip. They were sure of going. Anne was rather dubious at first, but Grace overruled her objections, and made fun of Jessica for saying she had promised to visit her aunt.

"Go and visit your aunt afterwards, Jessica. Remember, she is a secondary matter when compared to us," she said laughingly.

"I shall take my car," said Tom. "That will help things along."

"Mother has promised me one," remarked David, "so we'll have plenty of means of conveyance.

"How sorry I am that you can't go, too, Aunt Rose," exclaimed Tom regretfully.

"Nonsense," replied his aunt, "you don't want an old woman at your heels all the time. Besides, I must visit my brother in California this summer. I haven't seen him for several years."

"Let's drink to the success of the house party," cried Reddy, "and pledge ourselves to be on time next Tuesday morning. Drink her down."

When next we meet our Oakdale boys and girls, they will have returned to their books after a long happy summer. In "GRACE HARLOWE'S JUNIOR YEAR AT HIGH SCHOOL"; Or, "FAST FRIENDS IN THE SORORITIES," the girl chums will appear as members of a High School sorority. Here the reader will make the acquaintance of Eleanor Savell, a clever but exceedingly wilful girl, whose advent in Oakdale High School brings about a series of happenings that make the story one of absorbing interest. The doings of a rival sorority, organized by Eleanor, the contest for dramatic honors between Eleanor and Anne Pierson and the mischievous plot against the latter originated by the former and frustrated by Grace Harlowe, are among the features that will hold the attention and cement the reader's friendship for the girl chums.

Choose from Thousands of 1stWorldLibrary Classics By

A. M. Barnard
Ada Leverson
Adolphus William Ward
Aesop
Agatha Christie
Alexander Aaronsohn
Alexander Kielland
Alexandre Dumas
Alfred Gatty
Alfred Ollivant
Alice Duer Miller
Alice Turner Curtis
Alice Dunbar
Allen Chapman
Ambrose Bierce
Amelia E. Barr
Amory H. Bradford
Andrew Lang
Andrew McFarland Davis
Andy Adams
Anna Alice Chapin
Anna Sewell
Annie Besant
Annie Hamilton Donnell
Annie Payson Call
Annie Roe Carr
Annonaymous
Anton Chekhov
Arnold Bennett
Arthur Conan Doyle
Arthur M. Winfield
Arthur Ransome
Arthur Schnitzler
Atticus
B.H. Baden-Powell
B. M. Bower
B. C. Chatterjee
Baroness Emmuska Orczy
Baroness Orczy
Basil King
Bayard Taylor
Ben Macomber
Bertha Muzzy Bower
Bjornstjerne Bjornson
Booth Tarkington
Boyd Cable
Bram Stoker
C. Collodi
C. E. Orr

C. M. Ingleby
Carolyn Wells
Catherine Parr Traill
Charles A. Eastman
Charles Amory Beach
Charles Dickens
Charles Dudley Warner
Charles Farrar Browne
Charles Ives
Charles Kingsley
Charles Klein
Charles Hanson Towne
Charles Lathrop Pack
Charles Romyn Dake
Charles Whibley
Charles Willing Beale
Charlotte M. Braeme
Charlotte M. Yonge
Charlotte Perkins Stetson
Clair W. Hayes
Clarence Day Jr.
Clarence E. Mulford
Clemence Housman
Confucius
Coningsby Dawson
Cornelis DeWitt Wilcox
Cyril Burleigh
D. H. Lawrence
Daniel Defoe
David Garnett
Dinah Craik
Don Carlos Janes
Donald Keyhoe
Dorothy Kilner
Dougan Clark
Douglas Fairbanks
E. Nesbit
E.P.Roe
E. Phillips Oppenheim
Earl Barnes
Edgar Rice Burroughs
Edith Van Dyne
Edith Wharton
Edward Everett Hale
Edward J. O'Biren
Edward S. Ellis
Edwin L. Arnold
Eleanor Atkins
Eliot Gregory

Elizabeth Gaskell
Elizabeth McCracken
Elizabeth Von Arnim
Ellem Key
Emerson Hough
Emilie F. Carlen
Emily Dickinson
Enid Bagnold
Enilor Macartney Lane
Erasmus W. Jones
Ernie Howard Pie
Ethel May Dell
Ethel Turner
Ethel Watts Mumford
Eugenie Foa
Eugene Wood
Eustace Hale Ball
Evelyn Everett-green
Everard Cotes
F. H. Cheley
F. J. Cross
F. Marion Crawford
Federick Austin Ogg
Ferdinand Ossendowski
Francis Bacon
Francis Darwin
Frances Hodgson Burnett
Frances Parkinson Keyes
Frank Gee Patchin
Frank Harris
Frank Jewett Mather
Frank L. Packard
Frank V. Webster
Frederic Stewart Isham
Frederick Trevor Hill
Frederick Winslow Taylor
Friedrich Kerst
Friedrich Nietzsche
Fyodor Dostoyevsky
G.A. Henty
G.K. Chesterton
Gabrielle E. Jackson
Garrett P. Serviss
Gaston Leroux
George A. Warren
George Ade
Geroge Bernard Shaw
George Durston
George Ebers

George Eliot
George Gissing
George MacDonald
George Meredith
George Orwell
George Sylvester Viereck
George Tucker
George W. Cable
George Wharton James
Gertrude Atherton
Gordon Casserly
Grace E. King
Grace Gallatin
Grace Greenwood
Grant Allen
Guillermo A. Sherwell
Gulielma Zollinger
Gustav Flaubert
H. A. Cody
H. B. Irving
H.C. Bailey
H. G. Wells
H. H. Munro
H. Irving Hancock
H. Rider Haggard
H. W. C. Davis
Haldeman Julius
Hall Caine
Hamilton Wright Mabie
Hans Christian Andersen
Harold Avery
Harold McGrath
Harriet Beecher Stowe
Harry Castlemon
Harry Coghill
Harry Houidini
Hayden Carruth
Helent Hunt Jackson
Helen Nicolay
Hendrik Conscience
Hendy David Thoreau
Henri Barbusse
Henrik Ibsen
Henry Adams
Henry Ford
Henry Frost
Henry James
Henry Jones Ford
Henry Seton Merriman
Henry W Longfellow
Herbert A. Giles

Herbert Carter
Herbert N. Casson
Herman Hesse
Hildegard G. Frey
Homer
Honore De Balzac
Horace B. Day
Horace Walpole
Horatio Alger Jr.
Howard Pyle
Howard R. Garis
Hugh Lofting
Hugh Walpole
Humphry Ward
Ian Maclaren
Inez Haynes Gillmore
Irving Bacheller
Isabel Hornibrook
Israel Abrahams
Ivan Turgenev
J.G.Austin
J. Henri Fabre
J. M. Barrie
J. Macdonald Oxley
J. S. Fletcher
J. S. Knowles
J. Storer Clouston
Jack London
Jacob Abbott
James Allen
James Andrews
James Baldwin
James Branch Cabell
James DeMille
James Joyce
James Lane Allen
James Lane Allen
James Oliver Curwood
James Oppenheim
James Otis
James R. Driscoll
Jane Austen
Jane L. Stewart
Janet Aldridge
Jens Peter Jacobsen
Jerome K. Jerome
John Burroughs
John Cournos
John F. Kennedy
John Gay
John Glasworthy

John Habberton
John Joy Bell
John Kendrick Bangs
John Milton
John Philip Sousa
Jonas Lauritz Idemil Lie
Jonathan Swift
Joseph A. Altsheler
Joseph Carey
Joseph Conrad
Joseph E. Badger Jr
Joseph Hergesheimer
Joseph Jacobs
Jules Vernes
Julian Hawthrone
Julie A Lippmann
Justin Huntly McCarthy
Kakuzo Okakura
Kenneth Grahame
Kenneth McGaffey
Kate Langley Bosher
Kate Langley Bosher
Katherine Cecil Thurston
Katherine Stokes
L. A. Abbot
L. T. Meade
L. Frank Baum
Latta Griswold
Laura Dent Crane
Laura Lee Hope
Laurence Housman
Lawrence Beasley
Leo Tolstoy
Leonid Andreyev
Lewis Carroll
Lewis Sperry Chafer
Lilian Bell
Lloyd Osbourne
Louis Hughes
Louis Tracy
Louisa May Alcott
Lucy Fitch Perkins
Lucy Maud Montgomery
Luther Benson
Lydia Miller Middleton
Lyndon Orr
M. Corvus
M. H. Adams
Margaret E. Sangster
Margret Howth
Margaret Vandercook

Margret Penrose
Maria Edgeworth
Maria Thompson Daviess
Mariano Azuela
Marion Polk Angellotti
Mark Overton
Mark Twain
Mary Austin
Mary Catherine Crowley
Mary Cole
Mary Hastings Bradley
Mary Roberts Rinehart
Mary Rowlandson
M. Wollstonecraft Shelley
Maud Lindsay
Max Beerbohm
Myra Kelly
Nathaniel Hawthrone
Nicolo Machiavelli
O. F. Walton
Oscar Wilde
Owen Johnson
P.G. Wodehouse
Paul and Mabel Thorne
Paul G. Tomlinson
Paul Severing
Percy Brebner
Peter B. Kyne
Plato
R. Derby Holmes
R. L. Stevenson
R. S. Ball
Rabindranath Tagore
Rahul Alvares
Ralph Bonehill
Ralph Henry Barbour
Ralph Victor
Ralph Waldo Emmerson
Rene Descartes
Rex Beach

Rex E. Beach
Richard Harding Davis
Richard Jefferies
Richard Le Gallienne
Robert Barr
Robert Frost
Robert Gordon Anderson
Robert L. Drake
Robert Lansing
Robert Lynd
Robert Michael Ballantyne
Robert W. Chambers
Rosa Nouchette Carey
Rudyard Kipling
Samuel B. Allison
Samuel Hopkins Adams
Sarah Bernhardt
Sarah C. Hallowell
Selma Lagerlof
Sherwood Anderson
Sigmund Freud
Standish O'Grady
Stanley Weyman
Stella Benson
Stella M. Francis
Stephen Crane
Stewart Edward White
Stijn Streuvels
Swami Abhedananda
Swami Parmananda
T. S. Ackland
T. S. Arthur
The Princess Der Ling
Thomas A. Janvier
Thomas A Kempis
Thomas Anderton
Thomas Bailey Aldrich
Thomas Bulfinch
Thomas De Quincey
Thomas Dixon

Thomas H. Huxley
Thomas Hardy
Thomas More
Thornton W. Burgess
U. S. Grant
Valentine Williams
Various Authors
Vaughan Kester
Victor Appleton
Victoria Cross
Virginia Woolf
Wadsworth Camp
Walter Camp
Walter Scott
Washington Irving
Wilbur Lawton
Wilkie Collins
Willa Cather
Willard F. Baker
William Dean Howells
William le Queux
W. Makepeace Thackeray
William W. Walter
William Shakespeare
Winston Churchill
Yei Theodora Ozaki
Yogi Ramacharaka
Young E. Allison
Zane Grey

www.ingramcontent.com/pod-product-compliance
Lightning Source LLC
Chambersburg PA
CBHW020502100426
42813CB00030B/3086/J